echt 1

Symbols and headings you will find in the book – what do they mean?

Lesen — A reading activity

Hören — A listening activity

Schreiben — A writing activity

Sprechen — A speaking activity

Übersetzen — A translation activity

Kultur
Learn more about the culture of the German-speaking world

Sprachlabor
Grammar and pronunciation practice

Was kann ich schon?
Test what you have learnt

Vorankommen!
Reinforcement and extension activities

Vokabeln
Key vocabulary from the unit

Sprungbrett
Go further with exam-style activities

Grammatik
Grammar reference

Glossar
Glossary

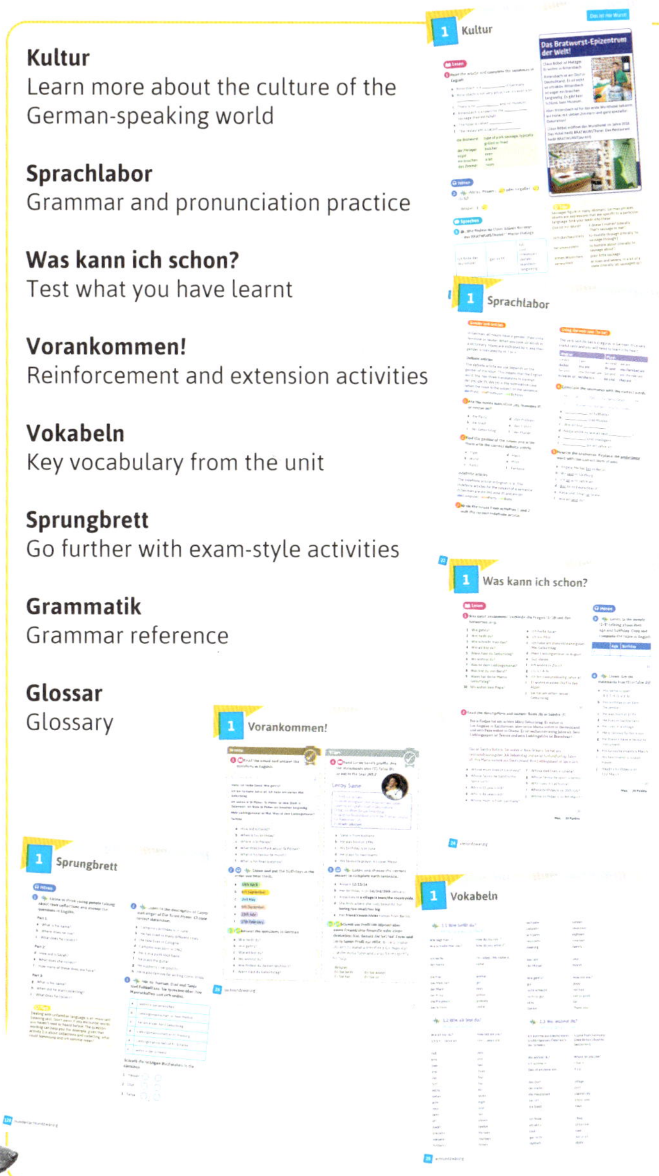

Grammatik
Grammar explanations

Strategie
Strategies for language learning

Sprachmuster
Language patterns

Extra
Extra challenges and tips for extending answers

Kultur
Information on the German-speaking world

Achtung!
Tips on avoiding mistakes

Aussprache
Tips on pronunciation

Tipp
Further hints

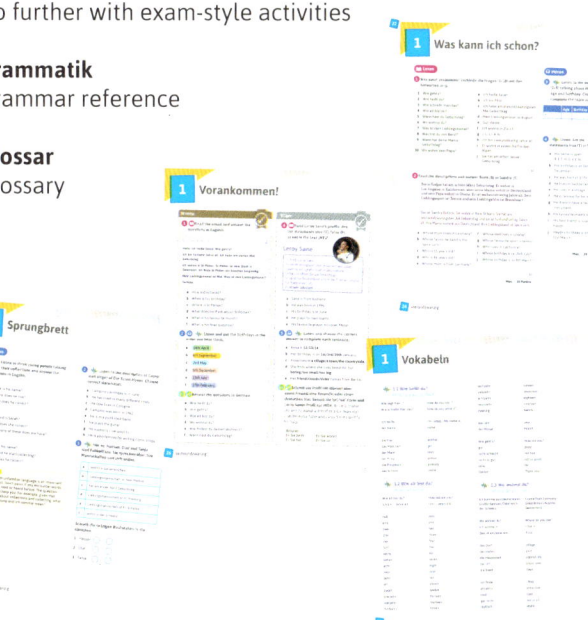

Anneli McLachlan
Mariela Affum
Marcus Waltl

Inhalt

Pages 4–7

Die deutschsprachige Welt... 4–5
In der Deutschstunde 6
Wichtige Wörter 7

Unit 1 Hallo!
Pages 8–29

Los geht's!

1.1 Wie heißt du?
- Introducing yourself
- Finding out about gender and articles

1.2 Wie alt bist du?
- Learning numbers 1–20
- Using the verb *sein* ('to be')

1.3 Wo wohnst du?
- Talking about where you live
- Using the verb *wohnen* ('to live')

1.4 Herzlichen Glückwunsch!
- Saying when your birthday is
- Using the verb *haben* ('to have')

1.5 Wer war das?
- Learning numbers 31–1000
- Identifying personal pronouns

Kultur
Das ist mir Wurst!

Sprachlabor

Was kann ich schon?

Vorankommen!

Vokabeln

Unit 2 Das ist meine Welt!
Pages 30–51

Los geht's!

2.1 Bei mir zu Hause
- Talking about family members
- Using *haben* with the accusative case

2.2 Wir sind Freunde
- Describing someone's personality
- Using possessive adjectives *mein* and *dein*

2.3 Was ist deine Lieblingsfarbe?
- Describing hair and eye colour
- Starting to recognise adjective endings

2.4 Alles bunt!
- Learning parts of the body
- Using conjunctions *und*, *aber* and *oder*

2.5 Was sind deine Lieblingstiere?
- Talking about pets and animals
- Forming plural nouns

Kultur
Deutsche Kinder- und Jugendliteratur

Sprachlabor

Was kann ich schon?

Vorankommen!

Vokabeln

Unit 3 Meine Freizeit
Pages 52–73

Los geht's!

3.1 Sport macht Spaß!
- Talking about sport
- Revising the present tense

3.2 Das mache ich gern!
- Talking about your hobbies
- Using irregular verbs

3.3 Hast du Zeit?
- Saying how often you do something
- Applying the 'verb-second' rule

3.4 Was für Musik hörst du gern?
- Talking about music you listen to and play
- Using (*gar nicht*) *gern*, *lieber*, *am liebsten*

3.5 Stars und Trends – was gibt's Neues?
- Talking about famous people and online life
- Starting to recognise different tenses

Kultur
Ich male gern!

Sprachlabor

Was kann ich schon?

Vorankommen!

Vokabeln

2 zwei

Unit 4 In der Schule
Pages 74–95

Los geht's!

4.1 Heute habe ich Geschichte!
- Talking about school subjects
- Telling the time

4.2 Mathe macht Spaß!
- Giving opinions of school subjects
- Using subordinate clauses with *weil*

4.3 Deutsch lernen – eine gute Idee!
- Talking about learning habits and teachers
- Using impersonal expressions

4.4 Was gibt es in deiner Schule?
- Talking about what your school is like
- Using *man* with modal verbs

4.5 Welche AG machst du?
- Talking about after-school activities
- Revising the 'verb-second' rule

Kultur
Schulleben in deutschsprachigen Ländern

Sprachlabor

Was kann ich schon?

Vorankommen!

Vokabeln

Unit 5 Mahlzeit!
Pages 96–117

Los geht's!

5.1 Frühstück – die wichtigste Mahlzeit!
- Talking about what you eat and drink
- Using the verbs *essen* and *trinken*

5.2 Wie schmeckt's?
- Buying food
- Using *mir* and *dir*

5.3 Foodtruck-Fieber!
- Ordering something to eat
- Using *ich möchte* and *ich hätte gern*

5.4 Guten Appetit!
- Reading restaurant reviews
- Starting to use the perfect tense with *haben*

5.5 Besser essen
- Talking about healthy eating
- Using *man soll*

Kultur
Eine kulinarische Reise

Sprachlabor

Was kann ich schon?

Vorankommen!

Vokabeln

Unit 6 Die Welt des Lesens
Pages 118–127

Los geht's!

6.1 Berühmte Autoren
- Getting to know German-speaking writers
- Revising the perfect tense with *haben*

6.2 Es war einmal…
- Learning about the German fairy tale tradition
- Starting to use the imperfect tense

Kultur
Das Leben der Anne Frank

Sprachlabor

Was kann ich schon?

Sprungbrett
Pages 128–137

Listening and Speaking (Units 1, 3, 5)
. . . . 128–129; 132–133; 136–137
Reading and Writing (Units 2, 4)
. . . . 130–131; 134–135

Pages 138–151

Grammatik 138–143
Glossar 144–151

Die deutschsprachige Welt

Sprichst du Deutsch?

German is the only official language in Germany, Austria and Liechtenstein.

German is also an official language in Switzerland, Belgium and Luxembourg.

Did you know that German is also spoken in parts of northern Italy?

The birthplace of gummy bears is **Bonn**, where Haribo's headquarters are based.

Cologne carnival is Germany's biggest party! Every year millions of people wear fancy dress and celebrate in the street.

The *Town Musicians of Bremen*, the story of four animals on their way to **Bremen** to start a new life, is just one of the many German folk stories and fairy tales published by the Brothers Grimm.

The *Hafengeburtstag* is a festival to celebrate the port of **Hamburg**, which is the largest in Germany. Every year a parade of 300 ships travels down the River Elbe.

Berlin is the capital of Germany. The Brandenburg Gate, an important monument, is a popular spot for selfies.

Neuschwanstein Castle in southern Bavaria was the inspiration for Disneyland's Sleeping Beauty Castle.

Bayern **Munich** is Germany's most successful football team. The top German male football league is called the *Bundesliga* and the women's league is called the *Frauen-Bundesliga*.

The waltz is a famous type of dance and music that became fashionable in **Vienna**. There are 450 balls a year in Vienna for dance fans!

The huge art museum in **Graz** is known as the 'friendly alien' because of the building's strange shape.

The **Alps** are the highest mountain range in Europe. The mountains stretch from Austria in the east to France in the west, covering parts of Italy, Switzerland and Germany in between.

No visit to **Switzerland** is complete without tasting famous Swiss chocolate or Swiss cheese. Try a cheese fondue: cubes of bread dipped in melted cheese. *Lecker!*

Alpine horns are several metres long! They were originally used by Swiss herders to call to their cows.

fünf 5

In der Deutschstunde

Instructions

Beantworte…	Answer…	…auf Deutsch.	…in/into German.
Benutzt…	Use…	…auf Englisch.	…in/into English.
Beschreib…	Describe…	…das Bild.	…the picture.
Bring … in die richtige Reihenfolge.	Put … in the correct order.	…das Kästchen.	…the box.
Erfinde…	Invent…	…die Buchstaben.	…the letters.
Finde…	Find…	…die Frage.	…the question.
Füll … aus.	Fill in/Complete…	…die Lücken.	…the gaps.
Gib…	Give…	…die Paare.	…the pairs.
Hör zu.	Listen.	…die passenden Bilder.	…the matching images.
Korrigiere…	Correct…	…die richtige Antwort.	…the correct answer.
Lies…	Read…	…die Sätze.	…the sentences.
Macht…	Make/Do…	…die Wörter.	…the words.
Notiere…	Make a note of…	…ein Interview.	…an interview.
Schau … an.	Look at…	…ein Rollenspiel.	…a roleplay.
Schreib…	Write…	…einen Artikel über…	…an article about…
Schreib … ab.	Copy…	…einen Blogeintrag.	…a blog post.
Sprich…	Speak/Talk…	…einen Dialog.	…a conversation.
Such…	Look for…	…einen Paragrafen.	…a paragraph.
Tauscht…	Swap…	…einen Text.	…a text.
Übersetz…	Translate…	…etwas über…	…something about…
Verbinde…	Link…	…folgende Details.	…the following details.
Wähl…	Choose…	…Informationen über…	…information about…
Wiederhole…	Repeat…		

Ich habe meinen/meine/mein … vergessen.
I've forgotten my…

Ich brauche einen/eine/ein…
I need a…

Haben wir Hausaufgaben?
Do we have homework?

Darf ich zur Toilette?
May I go to the toilet?

Welche Seite?
Which page?

Bitte wiederholen Sie das.
Please could you repeat that.

Wie sagt man…?
How do you say…?

Ich verstehe nicht.
I don't understand.

Fertig!
Ready!/Done!

Wichtige Wörter

Numbers

null	0
eins	1
zwei	2
drei	3
vier	4
fünf	5
sechs	6
sieben	7
acht	8
neun	9
zehn	10
elf	11
zwölf	12
dreizehn	13
vierzehn	14
fünfzehn	15
sechzehn	16
siebzehn	17
achtzehn	18
neunzehn	19
zwanzig	20
einundzwanzig	21
zweiundzwanzig	22
dreiundzwanzig	23
vierundzwanzig	24
fünfundzwanzig	25
sechsundzwanzig	26
siebenundzwanzig	27
achtundzwanzig	28
neunundzwanzig	29
dreißig	30
einunddreißig	31
zweiunddreißig	32
vierzig	40
fünfzig	50
sechzig	60
siebzig	70
achtzig	80
neunzig	90
hundert	100
hunderteins	101
zweihundert	200
tausend	1000

Greetings

Hallo!	*Hello!*
Guten Tag!	*Good day!*
Guten Morgen!	*Good morning!*
Guten Abend!	*Good evening!*
Wie geht's?	*How are you?*
Gut, danke.	*Good, thank you.*
Tschüss!	*Bye!*
Auf Wiedersehen!	*Goodbye!*

Telling the time

Es ist … Uhr.	*It's … o'clock.*
Es ist zwanzig nach…	*It's twenty past…*
Es ist zehn vor…	*It's ten to…*
Es ist Viertel vor/nach…	*It's quarter to/past…*
Es ist halb fünf.	*It's half past four ('half to five').*

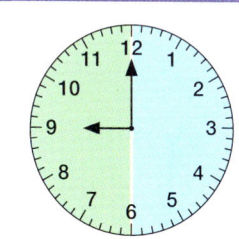

Conjunctions

und	*and*
aber	*but*
denn	*because*
oder	*or*
weil	*because*

Frequency words

nie	*never*
selten	*rarely*
ab und zu	*now and then*
manchmal	*sometimes*
oft	*often*
immer	*always*

Days of the week

Montag	*Monday*
Dienstag	*Tuesday*
Mittwoch	*Wednesday*
Donnerstag	*Thursday*
Freitag	*Friday*
Samstag	*Saturday*
Sonntag	*Sunday*

Intensifiers

besonders	*especially*
echt	*truly, really*
ein bisschen	*a little*
ganz	*completely*
gar nicht	*not at all*
mega (z.B. mega wichtig)	*super (e.g. super important)*
nicht so	*not very*
sehr	*very*
voll	*totally*
völlig	*completely*
ziemlich	*quite*
zu	*too*

Expressing opinions and preferences

Ich mag…	*I like…*
Ich mag (gar) nicht…	*I don't like… (at all)*
Das finde ich…	*I find it…*
Mir gefällt…	*I like…*
…interessiert mich.	*…interests me.*
Ich esse/trinke/spiele (nicht) gern…	*I (don't) like eating/drinking/playing…*
Ich esse/trinke/spiele lieber…	*I prefer eating/drinking/playing…*
Am liebsten esse/trinke/spiele ich…	*I like eating/drinking/playing … most of all.*

1 Hallo!
Los geht's!

> **Tipp**
> Every noun in German has a gender: masculine, feminine or neuter.
> *der* Zoo – masculine
> *die* Altstadt – feminine
> *das* Matterhorn – neuter
> Do you know any other languages in which nouns have a gender?

1 Match the words (1–9) to the attractions (a–i).

Example: **1** g

1. a zoo
2. a cathedral
3. a hanging bridge
4. a mountain
5. a medieval town
6. Krimml Worlds of Water
7. a waterfall
8. Mozart's house
9. Brandenburg Gate

🇩🇪 Die drei besten Attraktionen in Deutschland

a
Der Kölner Dom
Region: Nordrhein-Westfalen

b
Die Altstadt von Rothenburg ob der Tauber
Region: Bayern

c
Das Brandenburger Tor
Region: Berlin

🇨🇭 Die drei besten Attraktionen in der Schweiz

d
Der Rheinfall
Region: Schaffhausen/Zürich

e
Die Triftbrücke
Region: Bern

f
Das Matterhorn
Region: Wallis

🇦🇹 Die drei besten Attraktionen in Österreich

g
Der Alpenzoo Innsbruck
Region: Tirol

h
Die Krimmler WasserWelten
Region: Salzburg

i
Das Geburtshaus von Mozart
Region: Salzburg

1 Hallo!

2 Read about two major rivers that run through several German-speaking countries. Put the English translations in the correct order.

Example: **1** d, …

a *Donau* in German, 'Danube' in English: the Danube is Europe's second longest river.

b It begins in Switzerland in the Alps.

c It is 1233 kilometres long.

d The Rhine is the longest river in Germany.

e The Danube is 2850 kilometres long.

1
Der Rhein ist der längste Fluss Deutschlands.
Er beginnt in der Schweiz in den Alpen.
Er hat eine Länge von 1233 Kilometern.

2
'Donau' auf Deutsch, *Danube* auf Englisch:
Die Donau ist der zweitlängste Fluss Europas.
Die Donau hat eine Länge von 2850 Kilometern.

3 Can you find the two rivers in the map on page 4?

4 Which of these German words have you already come across? Choose three words and use each of them in a sentence in English.

- kaputt
- Muesli
- Poltergeist
- Rucksack
- Delikatessen
- Dachshund
- Kindergarten
- Doppelgänger
- Angst

5 Write a paragraph in English entitled 'Did you know…?', with fun facts about Germany and German-speaking countries. How many facts can you include?

The facts could be about:
- language
- attractions
- sport
- famous people
- ?

neun 9

1.1 Wie heißt du?

Objectives
- Introducing yourself
- Finding out about gender and articles
- Learning the German alphabet

🎧 Hören

1 Hör zu. Wie schreibt man das? *(How do you write it?)*

2 Hör zu. Wie heißen sie (1–6)? *(What are they called?)*

Beispiel: **1** c

a Markus   d Sara
b Kirsti   e Anton
c Neva   f Jordan

⚙ Strategie

Learning the German alphabet

Most words in German are pronounced as they are written, so learning sound-spelling links will get you off to a great start.

The letter 'ß' (called *scharfes 's'* or *Eszett*) does not exist in English. It is the equivalent of a double 's'. Listen for it in *ich heiße* ('I am called').

An *umlaut* (¨) can be added to the vowels *a*, *o* and *u*. When you learn a word with an umlaut, listen out for the way it changes the vowel sound, which you can also hear in the audio for activity 1.

💬 Sprechen

3 👥 Wie sagt man die Namen? *(How do you say the names?)*

Milan   Ida   Harper   Renesmee

Jule   Elias   Maxi   Patrik   Vera

🎁 Extra

Can you tell which of the names in activity 3 are typical for boys (*Jungennamen*) and which are typical for girls (*Mädchennamen*)? Some names are commonly used for both sexes (*Unisexnamen*).

🎧 Hören

4 Hör zu. Ist alles richtig? *(Is everything correct?)*

10 zehn

Lesen

5 🎵 Hör zu und lies.

Hallo! Wie heißt du?
Ich heiße Karl. Und du?
Ich heiße Karoline.

Der Prinz heißt Karl. Die Prinzessin heißt Karoline. Das Schloss heißt Schönschloss.

Grammatik
p.22; WB p.5

Gender and articles

All German nouns are masculine, feminine or neuter. The word for 'the' (the definite article) and the word for 'a/an' (the indefinite article) in German changes according to the gender of the noun that follows.

	Definite article ('the')	Indefinite article ('a/an')
Masculine	der Prinz	ein Prinz
Feminine	die Prinzessin	eine Prinzessin
Neuter	das Schloss	ein Schloss

For plural nouns, the definite article is *die*: **die** Prinzen, **die** Prinzessinnen, **die** Schlösser.

⚠ Achtung!

The gender of a noun does not necessarily correspond to the gender of a person. The German word for 'man' (*der Mann*) is masculine and 'woman' (*die Frau*) is feminine, but the German word for 'girl' (*das Mädchen*) is neuter.

Übersetzen

6 Übersetz die Sätze ins Deutsche.

a Hello. I'm called Maxi.
b What's your name?
c How do you spell it?
d What is the castle called?

Sprechen

7 👥 Macht Dialoge mit den Namen.

Samuel   Jeet   Hamza   Gloria

Hallo. Wie heißt du?
Hallo. Ich heiße Zala.
Wie schreibt man das?
Z-A-L-A.

elf 11

1.2 Wie alt bist du?

Objectives
- Learning numbers 1–20
- Using the verb *sein* ('to be')
- Translating basic phrases

🎧 Hören

1 Hör zu und wiederhole (*repeat*).

0 null	1 eins	2 zwei	3 drei	4 vier	5 fünf	6 sechs	7 sieben
8 acht	9 neun	10 zehn	11 elf	12 zwölf	13 dreizehn	14 vierzehn
15 fünfzehn	16 sechzehn	17 siebzehn	18 achtzehn	19 neunzehn	20 zwanzig

✏️ Schreiben

2 Füll die Lücken aus.

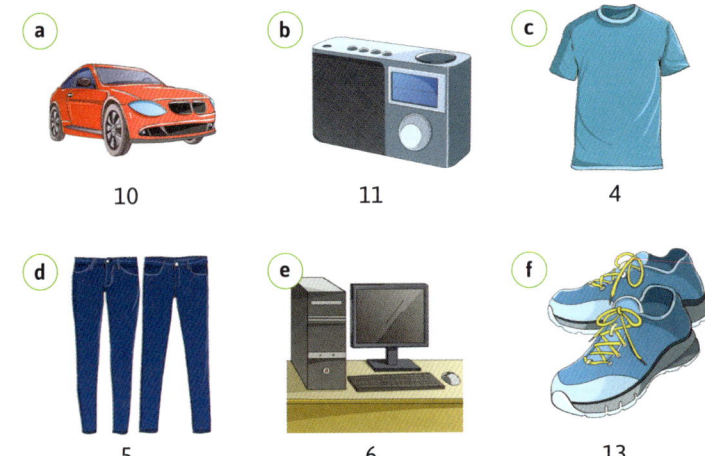

a — 10, b — 11, c — 4, d — 5, e — 6, f — 13

Beispiel: **a** Das Auto ist zehn Jahre alt.

a Das Auto ist _____ Jahre alt.
b Das Radio ist _____ Jahre alt.
c Das T-Shirt ist _____ Jahre alt.
d Die Jeans sind _____ Jahre alt.
e Der Computer ist _____ Jahre alt.
f Die Sneakers sind _____ Jahre alt.

🎧 Hören

3 Listen and answer. How old are Princess Karoline's possessions (1–5)? Make notes in English.

Example: **1** iPhone – three months old

dein/deine	your
mein/meine	my
Monate (pl)	months

Aa Grammatik   p.22; WB p.7

The present tense of *sein*

Singular		Plural	
ich bin	I am	wir sind	we are
du bist	you are	ihr seid	you (familiar) are
Sie sind	you (formal) are	Sie sind	you (formal) are
er/sie/es ist	he/she/it is	sie sind	they are

Wie alt bist du? (How old are you?)
Ich bin elf Jahre alt. (I am 11 years old.)

12 zwölf

1 Hallo!

💬 Sprechen

4 👥 **Macht Dialoge mit den Informationen.**

Casper, 13   Ella, 12

Sevda, 15   Ziad, 14

- Hallo. Wie heißt du?
- Hallo. Ich heiße _____ .
- Wie alt bist du?
- Ich bin _____ Jahre alt.

🎧 Hören

5 🎵 **Hör dir den Rap an. Mach mit!** (*Join in!*)

Alle zusammen! Alle zusammen!
Alle zusammen! Los!

Ich bin dreizehn.
Du bist vierzehn.
Er ist elf Jahre alt.
Sie ist acht.
Und wir sind sechzehn.
Ihr seid zwölf Jahre alt.
Sie sind zwanzig?
Sie sind siebzehn?
Das ist skandalös!

Wie alt bist du? Wie alt sind Sie?

Hallo, hallo. Wie alt sind sie?
Wie alt sind sie? Wie alt seid ihr?
Hallo, hallo. Wie alt sind wir?

📖 Lesen

6 **Welche Formen des Verbs 'sein' kannst du im Rap aus Aktivität 5 finden?**

Beispiel: ich bin, du bist, ...

🧩 Sprachmuster

Have you noticed that German has three different words for 'you', depending on how formal you need to be with the person you're talking to?

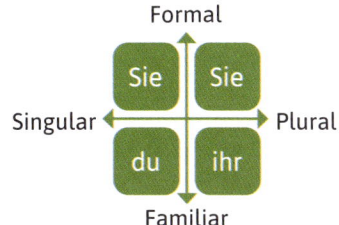

🎧 Hören

7 🎵 **Hör zu. Wie alt sind sie (1–5)?** (*How old are they?*) **Wie geht's ihnen?** (*How are they?*)

Beispiel: **1** 14, gut

Wie geht's?	How are you?
Gut!	🙂
Okay!/Nicht schlecht!	😐
Nicht so gut.	🙁
Danke!	Thank you!

🔄 Übersetzen

8 **Translate the conversation into English.**

- Hallo. Wie heißt du?
- Hallo. Ich heiße Prinz Karl.
- Wie alt bist du?
- Ich bin neunzehn Jahre alt.
- Wie geht's?
- Gut, danke!

⚙ Strategie

Translating basic phrases

Wie heißt du? literally means 'How are you called?' A good translation would be 'What are you called?' or 'What's your name?' Similarly, *Wie geht's?* means 'How goes it?' but we would say 'How are you?' in English. Don't just translate word for word – check that what you're writing sounds natural!

dreizehn **13**

1.3 Wo wohnst du?

Objectives
- Talking about where you live
- Using the verb *wohnen* ('to live')
- Reading aloud

Lesen

1 Listen and read the texts. Choose the correct answer to complete each sentence.

Hallo! Wie geht's?

Ich heiße Layla und ich bin achtzehn Jahre alt.

Ich wohne in Hamburg. Hamburg ist ein Hafen in Deutschland.

Ich finde Hamburg toll! So cool!

Guten Tag!

Ich bin Pablo. Ich bin dreizehn Jahre alt und ich komme aus der Schweiz.

Ich wohne in Bern – das ist die Hauptstadt.

Ich finde Bern attraktiv und gar nicht langweilig.

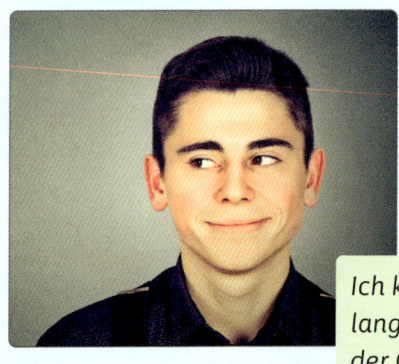

Servus! Wie geht's? Gut?

Ich heiße Sam. Ich wohne in Heiligenblut.

Heiligenblut ist ein Dorf in Österreich.

Im Winter ist Heiligenblut der perfekte Ort für Skifans!

Ich finde Heiligenblut idyllisch.

Ich komme aus	I come from
langweilig	boring
der Ort	place/area

a Layla lives in Hamburg. She is **18/19/20**.
b Hamburg is a **village/port/town**.
c Layla finds Hamburg **boring/attractive/cool**.
d Bern is in **Germany/Austria/Switzerland**.
e Pablo finds Bern **very/extremely/not at all** boring.
f Heiligenblut is a **village/port/town**.
g Heiligenblut is in **Germany/Austria/Switzerland**.
h Sam finds Heiligenblut **interesting/idyllic/cool**.

Strategie

Reading aloud

When you are reading, try saying the words aloud to yourself, using what you know about the links between sound and spelling in German. Don't be put off if you haven't seen a word before – if you say it aloud, you might be able to work out its meaning.

1 Hallo!

✏️ Schreiben

2 Füll die Lücken aus.

wohnen   wohnst   wohnen   wohne   wohnt

a Heidi _____ in einem Dorf in der Schweiz.
b Hänsel und Gretel _____ in einem Dorf in Deutschland.
c Wir _____ in Berlin. Berlin ist die Hauptstadt Deutschlands.
d Wo _____ du?
e Ich komme aus Österreich und _____ in Saarbrücken. Das ist eine Stadt.

🎧 Hören

3 Hör zu. Wo wohnen sie (1–4)?

Beispiel: **1** b

München

Wien

Alpbach

Bremerhaven

Aa Grammatik   p.23; WB p.9

The present tense of *wohnen*

The verb *wohnen* ('to live') is regular. To conjugate it, remove *-en* from the infinitive. This gives you the stem of the verb (*wohnen* → *wohn-*). Then add these endings:

Singular		Plural	
ich wohn**e**	I live	*wir* wohn**en**	we live
du wohn**st**	you live	*ihr* wohn**t**	you (familiar) live
Sie wohn**en**	you (formal) live	*Sie* wohn**en**	you (formal) live
er/sie/es wohn**t**	he/she/it lives	*sie* wohn**en**	they live

4 Listen again. What does each person (1–4) think of where they live? Make notes in English.

Example: **1** great, very cool, not at all boring

| toll | great |
| *es gefällt mir* | I like it (literally 'it pleases me') |

🌍 Kultur

In English, we use different names for many places to those used in German-speaking countries, for example Vienna is *Wien*, while Munich is *München*. Do you know any other examples?

💬 Sprechen

5 Macht Dialoge mit den Informationen.

Beispiel:
- Wie heißt du?
- Ich heiße Jessica.
- Wo wohnst du?
- Ich wohne in Grindelwald. Das ist ein Dorf in der Schweiz.
- Wie findest du Grindelwald?
- Ich finde es attraktiv!

Jessica – Grindelwald – ein Dorf – in der Schweiz – attraktiv

Sonja – Salzburg – eine Stadt – in Österreich – cool

Ari – Koblenz – eine Stadt – in Deutschland – langweilig

Thomas – Jena – eine Stadt – in Deutschland – toll

1.4 Herzlichen Glückwunsch!

Objectives
- Saying when your birthday is
- Using the verb *haben* ('to have')
- Comparing numbers in English and German

✏️ Schreiben

1 Füll die Lücken aus.

- 21 einundzwanzig
- 22 z_____iundzwanzig
- 23 dreiundzwan_____
- 24 v_____rundzwanzig
- 25 fü_____undzwanzig
- 26 se_____sundzwanzig
- 27 _____und_____nzig
- 28 acht_____
- 29 _____
- 30 dreißig

🎁 Extra

Using the pattern you spotted in activity 1, can you write out the numbers 31 to 39 in words in German?

2 Bring die Monate in die richtige Reihenfolge.

April   August   Februar   November   Januar
Juli   Juni   Mai   März   Dezember
Oktober   September

⚙️ Strategie

Comparing numbers in English and German

English is classed as a Germanic language, and so it has many similarities with German. Modern English comes from the Germanic dialects spoken by the Angles, the Saxons and the Jutes.

- Which German numbers from 1 to 10 do you think sound like the English numbers?
- Nineteen is *neunzehn*. What do you think 'teen' means in English?
- *Vierundzwanzig* literally translates as 'four and twenty'. Have you ever heard twenty-four expressed that way?

🎧 Hören

3 〰️ Hör zu. Ist alles richtig?

📖 Lesen

4 Wer ist das? Schreib den richtigen Namen.

3/1 Leon   26/4 Frieda   5/6 Melek

a. Wann hast du Geburtstag?
   Ich habe am fünften Juni Geburtstag.

b. Wann hast du Geburtstag?
   Ich habe am dritten Januar Geburtstag.

c. Wann hast du Geburtstag?
   Ich habe am sechsundzwanzigsten April Geburtstag.

🧩 Sprachmuster

A <u>cardinal</u> number ('one, two, three,…') says how many of something there are. An <u>ordinal</u> number ('first, second, third,…') tells you the position of something.

am ersten	on the first
am zweiten	on the second
am dritten	on the third
am siebten	on the seventh
am zwanzigsten	on the twentieth

Ordinal numbers in German are often given in short form: *am 7. Mai*.

1 Hallo!

🎧 Hören

5 〰️ Hör zu. Wann haben sie Geburtstag (1–8)? Finde die passenden Daten (a–h).

Beispiel: **1** h

1	Hannah	**a**	12/9
2	Ender	**b**	21/5
3	Jannik	**c**	4/3
4	Hamit	**d**	17/7
5	Sabrina	**e**	30/11
6	Tim	**f**	1/10
7	Elif	**g**	8/8
8	Serkan	**h**	9/12

Aa Grammatik p.23; WB p.11

The present tense of *haben*

Singular		Plural	
ich habe	I have	wir haben	we have
du hast	you have	ihr habt	you (familiar) have
Sie haben	you (formal) have	Sie haben	you (formal) have
er/sie/es hat	he/she/it has	sie haben	they have

✏️ Schreiben

6 Füll die Lücken aus.

a Wann _____ du Geburtstag?
b Ich _____ am zehnten April Geburtstag.
c Lisa _____ am siebten November Geburtstag.
d Wir _____ am achten August Geburtstag.
e In welchem Monat _____ Sie Geburtstag?

🔄 Übersetzen

7 Translate the sentences from activity 6 into English.

📖 Lesen

8 Read the article about Alexander Zverev. Are the statements true (T), false (F), or not in the text (NT)?

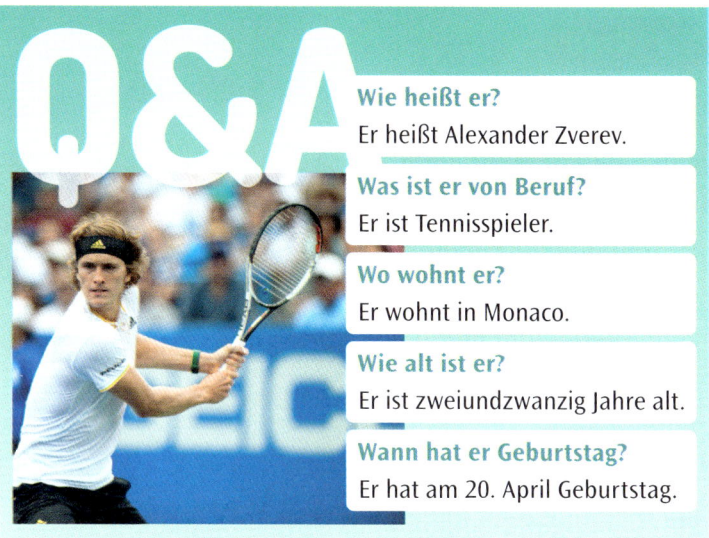

Q&A

Wie heißt er?
Er heißt Alexander Zverev.

Was ist er von Beruf?
Er ist Tennisspieler.

Wo wohnt er?
Er wohnt in Monaco.

Wie alt ist er?
Er ist zweiundzwanzig Jahre alt.

Wann hat er Geburtstag?
Er hat am 20. April Geburtstag.

Was ist er von Beruf?   What is his job?

a Alexander is a table tennis player.
b Alexander lives in Berlin.
c Alexander's birthday is on 20th April.
d His favourite month is April.
e Alexander is 32 years old.

💬 Sprechen

9 👥 Macht ein Exklusiv-Interview!

Name: Angela Merkel
Beruf: Politikerin
Wohnort: Berlin
Alter: 65
Geburtstag: 17/7

⚠️ **Achtung!**
For activity 9, use the *Sie* (formal 'you' form) for your questions and the *ich* form for your answers:
...heißen/sind/wohnen/haben Sie?
Ich heiße/bin/wohne/habe...

✏️ Schreiben

10 Schreib dein Interview aus Aktivität 9 auf.

Beispiel: Sie heißt ... und ist...

1.5 Wer war das?

Objectives
- Learning numbers 31–1000
- Identifying personal pronouns
- Using cognates to work out meaning

Lesen

1 Was passt zusammen?

1 Ich heiße Albert Einstein.
2 Ich habe am 14. März Geburtstag.
3 Ich bin Physiker.
4 Ich bin für die Relativitätstheorie bekannt.

a I'm a physicist.
b My name is Albert Einstein.
c I am known for the theory of relativity.
d My birthday is on 14th March.

Ich bin für ... bekannt. — I am known for...

Sprechen

2 Bringt die Zahlen in die richtige Reihenfolge.

einunddreißig   siebzig   neunzig   sechzig

dreihundert   vierzig   hundert   achtzig

fünfzig   zweihundert   tausend

Hören

3 Hör zu. Ist alles richtig?

Tipp
German numbers can be fun. You stick them together and they can end up being very long!
What is *neunzehnhundertsiebenundachtzig*?

Lesen

4 Finde die passenden Zahlen (*the matching numbers*).

1 312
2 4568
3 20 743
4 99
5 1111
6 62

a viertausendfünfhundertachtundsechzig
b neunundneunzig
c zwanzigtausendsiebenhundertdreiundvierzig
d tausendeinhundertelf
e dreihundertzwölf
f zweiundsechzig

Strategie

Using cognates to work out meaning

As German and English are both Germanic languages, you will find many 'cognates': words which look and sound similar in both languages. Together with your knowledge of context, these will help you to work out meaning.

- *Physiker* looks/sounds like...
- *Relativität* looks/sounds like...
- *Theorie* looks/sounds like...

Aussprache

The German *z* sound is pronounced 'ts', while the German single *s* is more like the softer English 'z'. Practise sounding as German as possible when you say numbers such as *siebzehn*, *sechzig* and *zweihundertsechs*.

1 Hallo!

🎧 Hören

5 Hör zu. Finde die passenden Jahre (*years*) (a–d).

Große Momente in Mathematik und Physik

1  **Die Relativitätstheorie ($E=mc^2$):** Am 25. November _____ entdeckt Albert Einstein die Relativitätstheorie.

2  **Schrödingers Katze:** Im Jahre _____ stellt Erwin Schrödinger seine Frage: Kann eine Katze lebendig und tot sein? In verschiedenen Welten…?

3  **Caroline Herschels Kometen:** Zwischen _____ entdeckt Caroline Herschel acht Kometen.

4 **Das Noether-Theorem:** Im Jahre _____ formuliert Emmy Noether das Noether-Theorem an der Universität Göttingen.

a 1786 und 1797
b 1918
c 1915
d 1935

entdeckt	discovers
die Katze	cat
lebendig	alive
tot	dead
in verschiedenen Welten	in different worlds
zwischen	between

Aa Grammatik   WB p.13

Personal pronouns

Personal pronouns take the place of specific nouns in sentences: for example, 'he' instead of 'the teacher', 'they' instead of 'Anna and Thomas'. Over the course of Unit 1, you have encountered these personal pronouns:

ich	I
du	you (familiar singular)
er	he
sie	she
es	it
wir	we
ihr	you (familiar plural)
Sie	you (formal singular/plural)
sie	they

Remember:
- *sie* with a lower case letter can mean 'she' or 'they'. The verb ending will depend on which of these it is.
- *Sie* with a capital letter is the formal word for 'you' (singular or plural). Use the familiar forms *du* (singular) or *ihr* (plural) when you don't need to be formal.

✏️ Schreiben

6 Schreib die Sätze aus Aktivität 1 in der 'er'-Form.

7 Wähl eine dieser Personen und schreib vier Sätze über ihn/sie. Benutz (*use*) 'er' oder 'sie'.

Beispiel: Sie heißt…

Name: Emmy Noether
Geburtstag: 23/3
Beruf: Mathematikerin
Bekannt für: das Noether-Theorem

Name: Erwin Schrödinger
Geburtstag: 12/8
Beruf: Physiker
Bekannt für: Schrödingers Katze

Name: Caroline Herschel
Geburtstag: 16/3
Beruf: Physikerin
Bekannt für: Kometen

neunzehn

1 Kultur

Das ist mir Wurst!

Das Bratwurst-Epizentrum der Welt!

Claus Böbel ist Metzger. Er wohnt in Rittersbach.

Rittersbach ist ein Dorf in Deutschland. Es ist nicht so attraktiv. Rittersbach ist sogar ein bisschen langweilig. Es gibt kein Schloss, kein Museum...

Aber Rittersbach ist für das erste Wursthotel bekannt: ein Hotel mit sieben Zimmern und ganz spezieller Dekoration!

Claus Böbel eröffnet das Wursthotel im Jahre 2018. Das Hotel heißt BRATWURSThotel. Das Restaurant heißt BRATWURST(aurant).

📖 Lesen

1 Read the article and complete the sentences in English.

a Rittersbach is a _____ in Germany.
b Rittersbach is not very attractive. It's even a bit _____ .
c There is no _____ and no museum.
d Rittersbach is known for the _____ sausage-themed hotel!
e The hotel is called _____ .
f The restaurant is called _____ .

die Bratwurst	type of pork sausage, typically grilled or fried
der Metzger	butcher
sogar	even
ein bisschen	a bit
das Zimmer	room

🎧 Hören

2 〰️ Hör zu. Positiv (🙂) oder negativ (😣) (1–5)?

Beispiel: 1 🙂

💡 Tipp

Sausages figure in many idiomatic German phrases. Idioms are expressions that are specific to a particular language. Sink your teeth into these!

Das ist mir Wurst!	It doesn't matter! (literally 'That's sausage to me!')
sich durchwursteln	to muddle through (literally 'to sausage through')
herumwursteln	to bumble about (literally 'to sausage about')
armes Würstchen	poor little sausage
verwurstelt	at sixes and sevens, in a bit of a state (literally 'all sausaged up')

💬 Sprechen

3 👥 „Wie findest du Claus Böbels Konzept – das BRATWURSThotel?" Macht Dialoge.

| Ich finde das Wursthotel | (gar nicht) | toll.
cool.
interessant.
perfekt.
skandalös.
langweilig. |

20 zwanzig

1 Hallo!

📖 Lesen

4 Lies den Artikel. Schreib Herta Heuwers Profil ab und füll es aus.

Currywurstkult!

Herta Heuwer hat am 13. Juni Geburtstag.

Sie wohnt in Berlin und arbeitet in einer Imbissbude.

Am 4. September 1949 macht Herta die erste Currywurst.

Die Deutschen essen jedes Jahr achthundert Millionen Currywürste.

Am 4. September ist der Tag der Currywurst.

die Currywurst	sliced sausage seasoned with curry ketchup and topped with curry powder
die Imbissbude	snack bar

Name: Herta Heuwer
Wohnort: _____
Geburtstag: _____
Arbeitet in: _____
Bekannt für: _____
Currywursttag: _____

Currywurst is attributed to Herta Heuwer from Berlin, but Lena Brücker from Hamburg claimed to have invented it in 1947! *Currywurst* is a German institution. Over 800 million are eaten each year!

🎧 Hören

5 Hör zu. Bring die Sätze (a–h) in die richtige Reihenfolge.

Beispiel: d, ...

Veggie Boom

a Am ersten Oktober ist Weltvegetariertag.
b Das ist rund 10% aller Deutschen.
c In Deutschland gibt es 42 Millionen Flexitarier.
d Es gibt jetzt acht Millionen Vegetarier in Deutschland.
e Flexitarier essen selten Fleisch oder Fisch.
f In Berlin allein gibt es rund 50 vegane oder vegetarische Restaurants und Cafés.
g Eine Milliarde Menschen weltweit leben vegan oder vegetarisch.
h Der Trend ist global.

rund	about, approximately
es gibt	there is/there are
das Fleisch	meat
selten	rarely

🔄 Übersetzen

6 Choose four sentences from activity 5 and translate them into English.

✏️ Schreiben

7 Schreib ein paar (*a few*) Sätze über das Hotel Sacher.

Was? Hotel Sacher
Wo? Wien – Stadt in Österreich
Bekannt für? Sachertorte

die Sachertorte	a rich chocolate cake invented in Vienna

Das Hotel heißt…
Das Hotel ist…
Das Hotel ist für … bekannt.
Ich finde das Konzept…

einundzwanzig

1 Sprachlabor

Gender and articles

In German, all nouns have a gender: masculine, feminine or neuter. When you look up words in a dictionary, nouns are indicated by *n*, and their gender is indicated by *m, f* or *n*.

Definite articles

The definite article we use depends on the gender of the noun. This means that the English word 'the' has three translations in German: *der* (m), *die* (f), *das* (n) in the nominative case (when the noun is the subject of the sentence): **der** Prinz, **die** Prinzessin, **das** Schloss.

1 Are the nouns masculine (m), feminine (f), or neuter (n)?

- a die Party
- b die Stadt
- c der Geburtstag
- d das Problem
- e das T-Shirt
- f der Planet

2 Find the gender of the nouns and write them with the correct definite article.

- a Tiger
- b Wurst
- c Radio
- d Haus
- e Pilot
- f Fantasie

Indefinite articles

The indefinite article in English is 'a'. The indefinite articles for the subject of a sentence in German are *ein* (m), *eine* (f) and *ein* (n): **ein** Computer, **eine** Party, **ein** Baby.

3 Write the nouns from activities 1 and 2 with the correct indefinite article.

Using the verb *sein* ('to be')

The verb *sein* (to be) is irregular in German. It's a very useful verb and you will need to learn it by heart.

Singular		Plural	
ich bin	I am	wir sind	we are
du bist	you are	ihr seid	you (familiar) are
Sie sind	you (formal) are	Sie sind	you (formal) are
er/sie/es ist	he/she/it is	sie sind	they are

4 Complete the sentences with the correct words.

du   Wir   Bastian Schweinsteiger   ihr

Ich   Xavier Naidoo und Helene Fischer

- a _____ ist Fußballer.
- b _____ sind Musiker.
- c Wie alt bist _____ ?
- d Nadja und Kim, wie alt seid _____ ?
- e _____ sind intelligent.
- f _____ bin elf Jahre alt.

5 Rewrite the sentences. Replace the underlined word with the correct form of *sein*.

- a Angela Merkel <u>bin</u> in Berlin.
- b Wir <u>seid</u> in Salzburg.
- c Ich <u>ist</u> acht Jahre alt.
- d <u>Bist</u> ihr in Deutschland?
- e Katja und Omar <u>ist</u> Skater.
- f Wie alt <u>seid</u> du?

1 Hallo!

Using the verb *wohnen* ('to live')

Verb endings change depending on the subject of the sentence (the person or thing you are talking about). To conjugate (form) a regular verb such as *wohnen*, first remove the *-en* ending from the infinitive. This gives you the stem of the verb: *wohnen* → *wohn-*.

Then add these endings to the stem:

Singular	Plural
ich ____e	wir ____en
du ____st	ihr ____t
Sie ____en	Sie ____en
er/sie/es ____t	sie ____en

6 Complete the sentences with the correct form of *wohnen*.

a Ich _____ in Wien.
b Wo _____ du?
c Der Prinz _____ im Schloss.
d Wir _____ in der Schweiz.
e Thomas und Aysha _____ in Berlin.
f Königin Elizabeth _____ im Buckingham Palace.

7 Translate the sentences into German.

a I live in Stuttgart.
b He lives in Austria.
c Where do you (*ihr*) live?
d We live in Basel.
e Hannah and Ali live in Hamburg.
f Angela Merkel lives in Berlin.

Using the verb *haben* ('to have')

Like *sein*, the verb *haben* ('to have') is another irregular verb which is used frequently in German.

Singular		Plural	
ich habe	I have	wir haben	we have
du hast	you have	ihr habt	you (familiar) have
Sie haben	you (formal) have	Sie haben	you (formal) have
er/sie/es hat	he/she/it has	sie haben	they have

8 Complete the sentences with the correct form of *haben*.

a Ich _____ am zehnten März Geburtstag.
b Wir _____ einen Computer.
c Rebecca _____ am ersten August Geburtstag.
d Wann _____ du Geburtstag?
e Susi und Svenja _____ grüne Sneakers.
f Wann _____ ihr Geburtstag?
g Helene Fischer _____ ein Konzert in Freiburg.

9 Match the beginning and ending of the sentences.

1 Antonio
2 Wir
3 Ich
4 Wann
5 Hast

a habt ihr Geburtstag?
b haben einen Mercedes.
c du einen Laptop?
d hat am zwanzigsten April Geburtstag.
e habe am zweiten September Geburtstag.

Aussprache: *ie* and *ei*

The letter combinations 'ie' and 'ei' are very common in German and, because they look similar, they can cause confusion. Try to remember this: 'ie' is pronounced like the English letter 'e', and 'ei' is pronounced like the English letter 'i' (i.e. the second letter does the talking!).

10 Listen and repeat. Then practise with your partner.

Wien   Heiko   ein   die   Kiel   Schweinsteiger

11 Practise saying the sentences.

1 Schweinsteiger ist ein Meister im Fußball.
2 Die Stadt Wien ist ein beliebtes Reiseziel.

1 Was kann ich schon?

📖 Lesen

1 Was passt zusammen? Verbinde die Fragen (1–10) mit den Antworten (a–j).

1. Wie geht's?
2. Wie heißt du?
3. Wie schreibt man das?
4. Wie alt bist du?
5. Wann hast du Geburtstag?
6. Wo wohnst du?
7. Was ist dein Lieblingsmonat?
8. Was bist du von Beruf?
9. Wann hat deine Mama Geburtstag?
10. Wo wohnt dein Papa?

a. Ich heiße Julian.
b. Ich bin Pilot.
c. Ich habe am dreiundzwanzigsten Mai Geburtstag.
d. Mein Lieblingsmonat ist August.
e. Gut, danke.
f. Ich wohne in Zürich.
g. J-U-L-I-A-N.
h. Ich bin zweiunddreißig Jahre alt.
i. Er wohnt in einem Dorf in den Alpen.
j. Sie hat am elften Januar Geburtstag.

✓ 10

2 Read the descriptions and answer Boris (B) or Sandra (S).

Boris Kodjoe hat am achten März Geburtstag. Er wohnt in Los Angeles in Kalifornien, aber seine Mama wohnt in Deutschland und sein Papa wohnt in Ghana. Er ist sechsundvierzig Jahre alt. Sein Lieblingssport ist Tennis und sein Lieblingsfilm ist *Braveheart*.

Das ist Sandra Bullock. Sie wohnt in New Orleans. Sie hat am sechsundzwanzigsten Juli Geburtstag und sie ist fünfundfünfzig Jahre alt. Ihre Mama kommt aus Deutschland. Ihre Lieblingsband ist *Spice Girls*.

a. Whose mum lives in Germany?
b. Whose favourite band is the *Spice Girls*?
c. Who is 55 years old?
d. Who is 46 years old?
e. Whose mum is from Germany?
f. Whose dad lives in Ghana?
g. Whose favourite sport is tennis?
h. Who lives in California?
i. Whose birthday is on 26th July?
j. Whose birthday is on 8th March?

✓ 10

Max. ✓ 20 Punkte

🎧 Hören

3 Listen to the people (1–5) talking about their age and birthday. Copy and complete the table in English.

	Age	Birthday
1		

✓ 10

4 Listen. Are the statements true (T) or false (F)?

a. His name is spelt B-E-T-H-O-V-E-N.
b. His birthday is on 16th December.
c. He was born in 1770.
d. He lives in Switzerland.
e. He lives in a village.
f. He is famous for his music.
g. He doesn't have a favourite instrument.
h. His favourite month is March.
i. His best friend is Joseph Haydn.
j. Haydn's birthday is on 31st March.

✓ 10

Max. ✓ 20 Punkte

1 Hallo!

✏️ Schreiben

5 Schreib die Geburtstage.

Beispiel: 21/3 → am einundzwanzigsten März

a 30/4   b 20/2   c 8/10   d 15/8   e 23/11

✓ 5

6 Bring die Wörter in die richtige Reihenfolge.

a hast Wann du Geburtstag?
b wohnst du Wo?
c bist du Wie alt?
d Ich am August dritten habe Geburtstag.
e wohne in Ich Stadt einer in Österreich.
f zwölf bin Ich Jahre alt.
g Ahmed vierzehn ist alt Jahre.
h wohnen in Wir der Schweiz.
i Geburtstag Eva hat Juli am zweiten.
j Lieblingsmonat ist Mein August.

✓ 10

7 Übersetz das Internetprofil ins Deutsche.

Hi. I'm called Lina. I'm 14 years old. My birthday is on 15th June. June is my favourite month! I live in Berlin.

✓ 5

Max. ✓ 20 Punkte

Deine Resultate

How many points did you get?

Ask your teacher for the answers. Write down your score out of a total of 20 for Reading. Then do the same for Listening and Writing.

Find the right combination of Bronze, Silver and Gold activities for you on pp.26–27!

Up to 6 points   Well done! Do the Bronze activity in the next section.

7–12 points   Great! Do the Silver activity in the next section.

13–20 points   Fantastic! Do the Gold activity in the next section.

fünfundzwanzig **25**

1 Vorankommen!

Bronze

1 Read the email and answer the questions in English.

> Von: david@echtemail.de
>
> Hallo! Ich heiße David. Wie geht's?
>
> Ich bin fünfzehn Jahre alt. Ich habe am vierten Mai Geburtstag.
>
> Ich wohne in St Pölten. St Pölten ist eine Stadt in Österreich. Ich finde St Pölten ein bisschen langweilig.
>
> Mein Lieblingsmonat ist Mai. Was ist dein Lieblingsmonat?
>
> Tschüss

a How old is David?
b When is his birthday?
c Where is St Pölten?
d What does he think about St Pölten?
e What is his favourite month?
f What is his final question?

2 Listen and put the birthdays in the order you hear them.

a 14th April
b 6th September
c 2nd May
d 5th December
e 13th July
f 27th February

3 Answer the questions in German.

a Wie heißt du?
b Wie geht's?
c Wie alt bist du?
d Wo wohnst du?
e Wie findest du deinen Wohnort?
f Wann hast du Geburtstag?

Silber

4 Read Leroy Sané's profile. Are the statements true (T), false (F), or not in the text (NT)?

Leroy Sané

> Er heißt Leroy Sané.
> Er wohnt in England, aber er kommt aus Essen.
> Essen ist eine große Stadt in Deutschland.
> Er hat am elften Januar Geburtstag.
> Er spielt für Deutschland und in der Premier League für Manchester City.
> Er ist sehr talentiert.

a Sané is from Koblenz.
b He was born in 1996.
c His birthday is in June.
d He plays for two teams.
e His favourite player is Lionel Messi.

5 Listen and choose the correct answer to complete each sentence.

a Anna is **12/13/14**.
b Her birthday is on **1st/3rd/20th** January.
c Anna lives in **a village/a town/the countryside**.
d She finds where she lives beautiful but **boring/too small/too big**.
e Her **friend/cousin/sister** comes from Berlin.

6 Schreib ein Profil (40 Wörter) über einen Freund/eine Freundin oder einen deutschen Star. Benutz die 'er'/'sie'-Form und Leroy Sanés Profil zur Hilfe. Write a profile (40 words) about a friend or a German star. Use the er/sie form and Leroy Sané's profile for help.

> Beispiel:
> Er/Sie heißt...   Er/Sie wohnt...
> Er/Sie hat...   Er/Sie ist...

Gold

7 📖 **Lies den Blogeintrag und beantworte die Fragen auf Englisch.**

Hallo!

Ich heiße Kassim. Ich bin siebzehn Jahre alt und ich wohne in Wien in Österreich. Wien ist die Hauptstadt von Österreich.

Ich finde Wien total charmant! Wien ist historisch aber auch modern. Eine internationale Metropole. Ich finde diese Stadt supercool. Gefällt mir! :)

Wien ist die Weltstadt der Musik und die Wiener Kaffeehauskultur ist auch sehr bekannt. Mein Lieblingskaffeehaus heißt „Café Mozart". Dieses Kaffeehaus ist über zweihundert Jahre alt! Perfekt!

a Where does Kassim live?
b How does he find his home town?
c Name <u>one</u> thing his town is famous for.
d Which favourite place does he mention?
e How old is this place?

8 🎧 〰️ **Hör zu. Bastian beschreibt einen Freund. Wähl die <u>drei</u> richtigen Sätze.**

a Lutz is 14 years old.
b His birthday is in the summer.
c Lutz lives in Switzerland.
d He used to live in Liechtenstein.
e His house is very small.
f He has two brothers and three sisters.

9 ✏️ **Übersetz die Sätze ins Deutsche.**

a Vienna is known for music.
b I find Düsseldorf a bit boring.
c Berlin is charming.
d I come from Berlin.
e My favourite café is in Paris.

10 ✏️ **Beschreib deine Lieblingsstadt (60–80 Wörter).**

Schreib:

- wie die Stadt heißt
- deine Meinung über die Stadt
- wofür die Stadt bekannt ist
- noch ein Detail über die Stadt.

🎁 Extra

Try to include as many details as you can in your writing.

- Express opinions using the adjectives you know (*Es ist…/Ich finde…*).
- Give details about other people using your knowledge of verb endings (*Er/Sie heißt/ist/hat/wohnt… Sie heißen/sind/haben/wohnen…*).
- Use conjunctions to create longer sentences:
  und and *denn* because
  aber but

1 Vokabeln

1.1 Wie heißt du?
What are you called?

Wie sagt man…?	How do you say…?
Wie schreibt man das?	How do you write it?
Ich heiße…	I'm called…/My name is…
der Name	name
die Frau	woman
das Mädchen	girl
der Mann	man
der Prinz	prince
die Prinzessin	princess
das Schloss	castle

1.2 Wie alt bist du?
How old are you?

Wie alt bist du?	How old are you?
Ich bin … Jahre alt.	I am … years old.
null	zero
eins	one
zwei	two
drei	three
vier	four
fünf	five
sechs	six
sieben	seven
acht	eight
neun	nine
zehn	ten
elf	eleven
zwölf	twelve
dreizehn	thirteen
vierzehn	fourteen
fünfzehn	fifteen
sechzehn	sixteen
siebzehn	seventeen
achtzehn	eighteen
neunzehn	nineteen
zwanzig	twenty
das Jahr	year
der Monat	month
Wie geht's?	How are you?
gut	good
nicht schlecht	not bad
nicht so gut	not so good
okay	OK
Danke!	Thank you!

1.3 Wo wohnst du?
Where do you live?

Ich komme aus Deutschland/Großbritannien/Österreich/der Schweiz.	I come from Germany/Great Britain/Austria/Switzerland.
Wo wohnst du?	Where do you live?
Ich wohne in…	I live in…
Das ist ein/eine/ein…	It's a…
das Dorf	village
der Hafen	port
die Hauptstadt	capital city
der Ort	place/area
die Stadt	town
Ich finde…	I find…
attraktiv	attractive
cool	cool
gar nicht	not at all
idyllisch	idyllic

28 achtundzwanzig

interessant	interesting
langweilig	boring
toll	great
Es gefällt mir.	I like it.

1.4 Herzlichen Glückwunsch!
Happy Birthday!

einundzwanzig	twenty-one
zweiundzwanzig	twenty-two
dreiundzwanzig	twenty-three
vierundzwanzig	twenty-four
fünfundzwanzig	twenty-five
sechsundzwanzig	twenty-six
siebenundzwanzig	twenty-seven
achtundzwanzig	twenty-eight
neunundzwanzig	twenty-nine
dreißig	thirty
Wann hast du Geburtstag?	When is your birthday?
Ich habe am … Geburtstag.	My birthday is on the…
am ersten	on the first
am zweiten	on the second
am dritten	on the third
Januar	January
Februar	February
März	March
April	April
Mai	May
Juni	June
Juli	July
August	August
September	September
Oktober	October
November	November
Dezember	December

1.5 Wer war das?
Who was that?

einunddreißig	thirty-one
vierzig	forty
fünfzig	fifty
sechzig	sixty
siebzig	seventy
achtzig	eighty
neunzig	ninety
hundert	hundred/one hundred
zweihundert	two hundred
dreihundert	three hundred
tausend	thousand/one thousand
Ich bin für … bekannt.	I am known for…
der/die Mathematiker/Mathematikerin	mathematician
der/die Physiker/Physikerin	physicist

2 Das ist meine Welt!
Los geht's!

1 Im Tiergarten. Welches Tier ist das?

der Panda   der Seehund   das Zebra   das Walross   die Giraffe   das Krokodil

2 Wie viele Tiere gibt es? Was passt zusammen?

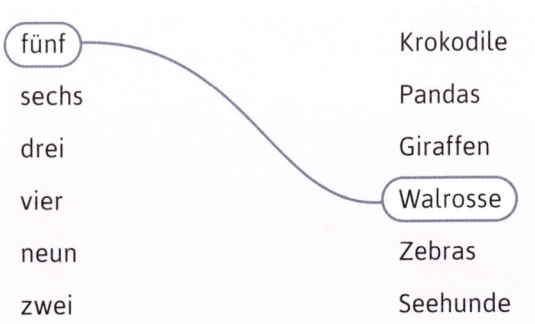

fünf	Krokodile
sechs	Pandas
drei	Giraffen
vier	Walrosse
neun	Zebras
zwei	Seehunde

> **Sprachmuster**
>
> German often puts two or more nouns together to make one long word. These are called 'compound nouns'.
>
> - *Tier* = animal
> - *Garten* = garden
> - *Tiergarten* = 'animal garden' = zoo
>
> Can you find three other compound nouns on these pages?

2 Das ist meine Welt!

3 Lies die Fakten über die Tiere aus Aktivitäten 1 und 2. Füll die Lücken aus.

Zebras   Seehunde   Krokodile   Giraffen   Walrosse   Pandas

a _____ kommen aus Afrika. Sie sind extrem groß.
b _____ sind schwarz und weiß und essen Bambus.
c _____ sind normalerweise braun oder grau. Sie sind freundlich.
d _____ sind lang und grün. Achtung, sie sind aggressive Reptilien!
e _____ sind groß und fett. Sie haben einen Schnurrbart und zwei lange Zähne.
f _____ haben schwarze und weiße Streifen.

4 Which five colours are mentioned in the facts in activity 3?

5 Welches Land repräsentiert die Fahne (*which country does the flag represent*): Deutschland, Österreich oder die Schweiz?

🗣 Kultur

The eagle is the national animal in both Germany and Austria. In Switzerland, there is no national animal.

Did you know that the Swiss flag is square?

rot
weiß
rot

schwarz
rot
gold

rot mit einem weißen Kreuz

6 👥 Persönlichkeitstest! „Welches Tier bist du?" Macht Dialoge.

Beispiel:
- Welches Tier bist du?
- Ich habe am 21. Februar Geburtstag. Ich bin der Elefant. Ich bin sozial und freundlich.

Ich bin	der Elefant.
	der Wolf.
	der Hund.
	der Bär.

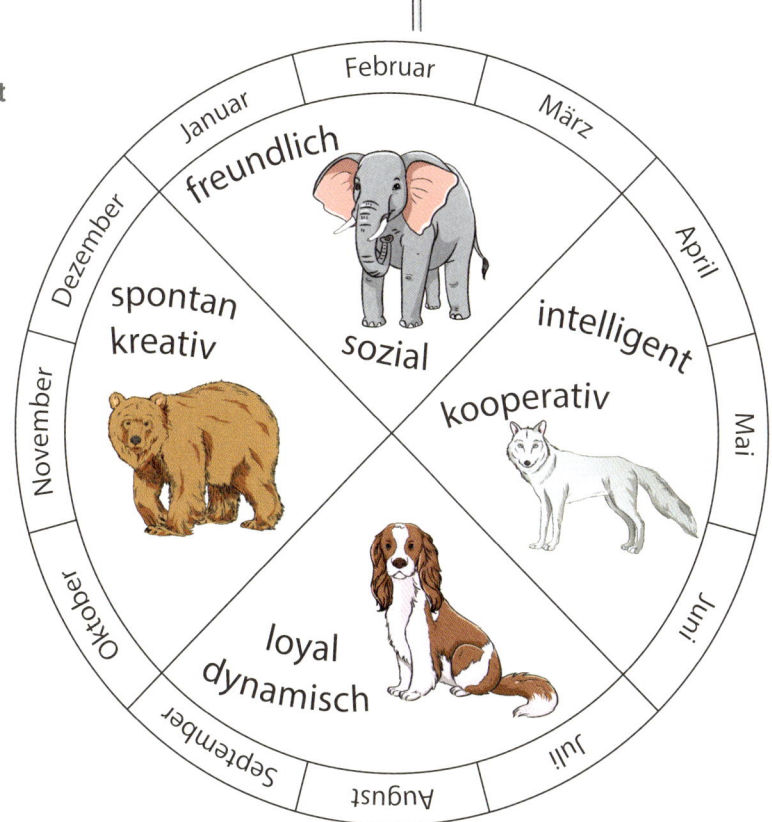

einunddreißig 31

2.1 Bei mir zu Hause

Objectives
- Talking about family members
- Using *haben* with the accusative case
- Recycling language

📖 Lesen

1 Was passt zusammen? Verbinde die Sätze (1–6) mit den Bildern (a–f).

1 Ich habe einen Bruder. Er heißt Hänsel.
2 Ich habe zwei Stiefschwestern.
3 Ich bin Einzelkind. Ich besuche meine Oma.
4 Ich habe sechs Brüder.
5 Ich habe keine Geschwister. Ich warte auf einen Prinzen.
6 Meine Schwester heißt Rosenrot. Wir sind Zwillinge.

 Aschenputtel

 Hänsel und Gretel

 Rotkäppchen

 Schneewittchen und die sieben Zwerge

 Schneeweißchen und Rosenrot

 Dornröschen

🎭 Kultur
The Grimm Brothers, Jacob (1785–1863) and Wilhelm (1786–1859), collected and published some of the best-known folk and fairy tales. Can you work out the English titles for the stories in activity 1?

🎧 Hören

2 Listen to the conversations. How many brothers and/or sisters does each person (1–4) have?

Example: 1 one sister, two brothers

💬 Sprechen

3 „Hast du Geschwister?" Macht Dialoge.

Ja, ich habe	einen Bruder/zwei Brüder. eine Schwester/zwei Schwestern.
Nein, ich habe	keinen Bruder/keine Schwester/ keine Geschwister.
Nein, ich bin	Einzelkind.

Aa Grammatik   p.44; WB p.15

Using the verb *haben*

After *ich habe*, the German word for 'a' adds *-en* when the noun is masculine:

ein Bruder (m) → *Ich habe ein**en** Bruder.*

To talk about something you don't have, use *kein* ('no', 'not any') in the same way.

Sprachmuster

You can add *Halb-* ('half') or *Stief-* ('step') to the words for family members:

*Ich habe eine **Halb**schwester.*

*Das ist mein **Stief**vater.*

For a twin sibling, add *Zwillings-* to *Bruder* or *Schwester*:

*Wir sind Zwillinge. Er ist mein **Zwillings**bruder.*

32 zweiunddreißig

2 Das ist meine Welt!

📖 Lesen

Eine typische Familie in Deutschland

Was bedeutet „typisch"?
Familie als Vater, Mutter, zwei Kinder: Das ist das typische Familienmodell. Es gibt aber andere Familientypen.
Die 'normale' Kleinfamilie (Mama, Papa, Kind) ist heute nicht die Norm.
Patchworkfamilien existieren: eine Mutter bringt ihre Kinder mit, oder ein Vater bringt seine Kinder mit und alle leben zusammen.
Regenbogenfamilien gibt es auch: Familien mit zwei Müttern oder zwei Vätern.

Was bedeutet…?   What does … mean?

4 Lies den Artikel und finde die passenden Wörter (a–d) auf Deutsch.

a family model
b blended families
c everyone lives together
d rainbow families

5 Read the article again. Are the statements true (T) or false (F)?

a A father, a mother and three children is a typical family.
b Families with one child are no longer the norm.
c Blended families don't live together.

🔄 Übersetzen

6 Übersetz die Sätze ins Deutsche.

a I have three sisters and one brother.
b Do you (*du*) have brothers and sisters?
c I have one sister. She is six years old.
d I have two brothers. They are called Mehmet and Hassan.

⚙ Strategie

Recycling language

Every week you should try to reuse language you have learnt before. For example, when talking about how many brothers or sisters you have, add details using language you already know by giving their names, ages and birthdays.

✏ Schreiben

7 Schreib drei oder vier Sätze über deine Familie oder eine andere Familie.

> Ich heiße Wilhelm Grimm. Das ist mein Bruder Jacob. Er hat am vierten Januar Geburtstag. Jacob und ich haben drei Brüder und eine Schwester, Charlotte.

💬 Sprechen

8 👥 Deck deine Sätze aus Aktivität 7 zu (*cover your sentences from activity 7*) und sprich über deine Familie. Dein Partner/Deine Partnerin schreibt alles auf Englisch auf.

dreiunddreißig

2.2 Wir sind Freunde

Objectives
- Describing someone's personality
- Using possessive adjectives *mein* and *dein*
- Using a bilingual dictionary

🎧 Hören

1 Hör zu. Wie sind die Freunde (1–5)? Finde die richtigen Adjektive (a–n).

Beispiel: **1** c, h

Wie ist dein bester Freund?
Wie ist deine beste Freundin?

a	dynamisch	h	lustig
b	kreativ	i	optimistisch
c	intelligent	j	freundlich
d	schüchtern	k	frech
e	egoistisch	l	langweilig
f	treu	m	respektvoll
g	faul	n	launisch

📖 Lesen

2 Check the meaning of the adjectives in activity 1 in a bilingual dictionary or in the wordlist on page 50.

⚙ Strategie
Using a bilingual dictionary

When you look up a German word, be careful with spelling and make sure you know how nouns, verbs, adjectives, etc. are labelled. The dictionary may give several meanings – decide which is the most relevant to the context.

💬 Sprechen

3 Schreib fünf Adjektive für einen Freund/eine Freundin. Dein Partner/Deine Partnerin muss raten (*has to guess*).

- Dein Freund ist kreativ.
- Ja, mein Freund ist kreativ.
- Deine Freundin ist schüchtern.
- Nein, meine Freundin ist nicht schüchtern.

Aa Grammatik p.44; WB p.17
Possessive adjectives

The words for 'my' and 'your' change when the noun that follows is feminine or a plural.

Das ist...
...*mein/dein* Freund/Vater/Bruder.
...*meine/deine* Freundin/Schwester/Mutter.

Das sind...
...*meine/deine* Freunde/Eltern/Großeltern.

2 Das ist meine Welt!

📖 Lesen

4 🎵 Listen and read the opinions about the qualities that are important in good friends. Copy and complete the table in English.

Name	Adjective	Intensifier (− / + / ++)
Nelli	respectful	++

Gute Freunde sind respektvoll. Das ist sehr positiv.
Nelli

Für mich ist ein guter Freund dynamisch. Das ist ziemlich positiv.
Gala

Gute Freunde sind nicht egoistisch. Das finde ich gar nicht positiv.
Julia

Meine beste Freundin ist lustig. Das ist sehr positiv.
Patrick

Für mich ist ein guter Freund nicht langweilig. Langweilig sein ist gar nicht positiv.
Jorvin

langweilig sein   being boring

🧩 Sprachmuster

Add intensifiers to make adjectives stronger or weaker:

++	sehr	very
+	ziemlich	quite, fairly
−	gar nicht	not at all

Another useful expression is *ein bisschen* ('a bit'), which you can use to soften a negative opinion:

Er ist ein bisschen egoistisch.

🔄 Übersetzen

5 Translate the text into English.

Ich bin lustig. Meine Schwester ist ziemlich lustig und mein bester Freund ist auch sehr lustig. Wir sind alle lustig! Das ist sehr positiv! Wie bist du?

✏️ Schreiben

6 Wähl sechs Adjektive aus. Schreib Sätze mit *sehr*, *ziemlich* oder *gar nicht*.

Beispiel: Gute Freunde sind nicht launisch. Das ist gar nicht positiv!

7 Du bist Ron Weasley. Beschreib deine Familie und deine Freunde.

Meine Schwester heißt Ginny. Sie ist...
Mein Vater heißt... Er ist...
Mein bester Freund heißt Harry. Er ist...

🎁 Extra

Now replace *positiv* with *negativ* in your sentences from activity 6.

Gute Freunde sind nicht launisch. Das ist sehr negativ! :(

fünfunddreißig **35**

2.3 Was ist deine Lieblingsfarbe?

Objectives
- Describing hair and eye colour
- Starting to recognise adjective endings
- Describing a photo

🎧 Hören

1 Listen and write each person's favourite colour (1–5).

Example: **1** *blue*

weiß orange grün schwarz gelb

blau braun grau violett rot

💬 Sprechen

2 „Was ist deine Lieblingsfarbe?" Macht Dialoge.

📖 Lesen

3 Wie sieht er/sie aus? Finde die passenden Bilder (a–f).

1. Sie hat mittellange blaue Haare und blaue Augen.
2. Er hat lange grüne Haare und braune Augen.
3. Sie hat kurze schwarze Haare und grüne Augen.
4. Sie hat lockige blonde Haare und rote Augen.
5. Er hat glatte graue Haare, einen Schnurrbart und braune Augen.
6. Er hat einen Bart, grüne Augen und Sommersprossen.

🎧 Hören

4 Hör zu. Ist alles richtig?

⚙ Strategie

Describing a photo

Wie sieht er/sie aus? (What does he/she look like?) This question often comes up when you are asked to describe people, for example in a photo. Use the language you know to give as much detail as you can. As well as describing hair and eyes, you can speculate about personality, e.g. *Sie sieht ziemlich schüchtern aus.*

Aa Grammatik WB p.19

Adjective endings

Adjectives change in German when they come before the noun they describe:

Meine Haare sind blau. → *Ich habe blau**e** Haare.*

Note that, when talking about hair, it is more common to use the plural *Haare* in German.

2 Das ist meine Welt!

Lesen

5 Listen and read the story about two people who meet at a holiday camp. Choose the correct answer to complete each sentence.

a Two **girls/boys** are spending their summer holidays at a camp.
b Luise is **moody/practical**. Lotte is **moody/practical**.
c Lotte lives in **Munich/Vienna** with her mother.
d Lotte und Luise are **twins/cousins**.
e After the camp, the girls swap **places/phone numbers**.

Kultur

Erich Kästner wrote *Das doppelte Lottchen* in 1949. It has been made into a film several times. The most famous recent version was entitled *The Parent Trap*. Have you seen it?

Das doppelte Lottchen

Zwei Mädchen verbringen die Sommerferien in einem Ferienlager.

<u>Luise Palfy hat lockige blonde Haare und ist neun Jahre alt. Lotte Körner hat auch lockige blonde Haare und ist auch neun Jahre alt. Luise ist launisch; Lotte ist praktisch.</u>

Luise und Lotte haben beide am vierzehnten Oktober Geburtstag. Beide sind in Linz geboren. Lotte und Luise sind Zwillinge! Sie wurden als Babys getrennt.

Ihre Eltern wohnen nicht mehr zusammen. Lotte wohnt bei ihrer Mutter in München; Luise wohnt bei ihrem Vater in Wien.

Lotte und Luise wollen wieder eine Familie sein. Nach den Ferien tauschen die Mädchen die Plätze. Lotte fährt als Luise nach Wien; Luise fährt als Lotte nach München.

Was könnte schief gehen?

beide	both
sie wurden als Babys getrennt	they were separated at birth
ihre Eltern	their parents
(sie) tauschen die Plätze	(they) swap places
Was könnte schief gehen?	What could go wrong?

Schreiben

6 Schreib die Identitätskarte für Luise und Lotte ab. Füll die Karte mit den richtigen Details aus.

Namen: Luise Palfy und Lotte Körner

Wie sehen sie aus?: _____

Alter: _____

Geburtstag: _____

Geburtsort: _____

Übersetzen

7 Translate the underlined paragraph of *Das doppelte Lottchen* into English.

Schreiben

8 Lindsay Lohan spielt beide Zwillingsschwestern im Film *The Parent Trap*. Schreib Sätze über das Foto.

- Wie sind ihre Haare? (*Sie hat…*)
- Wie sind ihre Augen? (*Sie hat…*)
- Findest du, sie sieht launisch oder praktisch aus? (*Sie sieht ziemlich/sehr/gar nicht … aus.*)

siebenunddreißig 37

2.4 Alles bunt!

Objectives
- Learning parts of the body
- Using conjunctions *und*, *aber* and *oder*
- Memorising new vocabulary

📖 Lesen

1 Jasper und Sabrina sind auf dem Holi-Festival. Schreib die Tabelle ab und füll sie aus.

der	die	das	die (plural)
der Kopf	die Hand	das Gesicht	die Ohren

Labels on Jasper (left): der Kopf, die Ohren, die Nase, die Schulter, der Arm, der Fuß

Labels on Sabrina (right): das Gesicht, die Hand, der Rücken, der Ellenbogen, der Bauch, das Bein, das Knie

Jasper — **Sabrina**

🎧 Hören

2 Listen and write the body parts mentioned and what colour they are.

Example: nose – purple

💬 Sprechen

3 Wer bist du: Jasper oder Sabrina? Macht Dialoge.

- Meine Haare sind gelb.
- Du bist Jasper.
- Richtig!
- Mein Ellenbogen ist grün.
- Du bist Sabrina.
- Ja, das stimmt!

Kultur

Holi is an Indian festival that has become really popular in Germany. It is a festival of colours that takes place in early spring.

38 achtunddreißig

2 Das ist meine Welt!

📖 Lesen

4 Lies den Text und finde die passenden Sätze (a–d) auf Deutsch.

a He is quite small and muscular.
b She has freckles and she is good-looking.
c He's big/tall but not chubby.
d She's slim and her face is blue.

🧩 Sprachmuster

Earlier in the unit, you used 'my' and 'your': *mein(e)* and *dein(e)*. To say 'his' and 'her', use *sein(e)* and *ihr(e)*, which behave in exactly the same way.

⚙️ Strategie

Memorising new vocabulary

Try sorting new words into categories to help you remember them, such as positive and negative. You could also try:

- visualising and drawing the word
- finding an associated word to jog your memory, e.g. *Rucksack → der Rücken*
- testing yourself by covering up and recalling the word.

Ich kann meine Freunde nicht finden!

Wo ist Marko? Er ist ziemlich klein und muskulös. Sein Gesicht ist rot und gelb.

Und Laura? Sie ist schlank und ihr Gesicht ist blau.

Wo ist Ender? Er ist groß aber nicht pummelig. Sein Rücken ist orange.

Ich finde Audrey nicht! Sie hat Sommersprossen und sie ist gut aussehend. Ihr Gesicht ist violett und gelb und orange, oder vielleicht blau…

Hilfe!

vielleicht — perhaps

🔄 Übersetzen

5 Übersetz die Sätze ins Deutsche.

a She is small and thin.
b I am quite good-looking.
c She is very tall and has black hair.
d His eyes are blue or perhaps grey.

Aa Grammatik p.45; WB p.21

Using the conjunctions *und*, *aber* and *oder*

The following are really useful conjunctions for linking ideas to form longer sentences:

und	and
aber	but
oder	or

✏️ Schreiben

6 Wie sieht deine Lieblingsfilmfigur (*your favourite film character*) aus? Schreib vier Sätze auf Deutsch.

Er/Sie ist	sehr	groß/klein/pummelig/ schlank/muskulös/ gut aussehend	und… aber… oder…
	ziemlich		
	nicht so		
	gar nicht		

neununddreißig **39**

2.5 Was sind deine Lieblingstiere?

Objectives
- Talking about pets and animals
- Forming plural nouns
- Using sound-spelling links to work out meaning

🎧 Hören

1 〰️ Hör zu. Finde die passenden Haustiere im Bild (a–h) für die Dialoge (1–8).

Beispiel: **1** d

Labels in picture:
- a – der Kanarienvogel
- b – das Kaninchen
- c – das Pferd
- d – die Katze
- e – der Fisch
- f – die Schlange
- g – das Meerschweinchen
- h – der Hund

💬 Sprechen

2 👥 „Hast du ein Haustier?" Macht Dialoge.

Nein, ich habe	kein Haustier.
Ja, ich habe	einen Hund/einen Fisch/ einen Kanarienvogel.
	eine Katze/eine Schlange.
	ein Meerschweinchen/ein Pferd.

🎧 Hören

3 〰️ Listen. Which animal from activity 1 is mentioned (1–8)? How many are there?

Example: **1** four cats

Aa Grammatik   p.45; WB p.23

Forming plural nouns

In German, we form plural nouns in several ways, such as by adding -*e*, -*er*, -*n*, -*en* or -*nen* to the end of the word.

Some words gain an umlaut on the last *a*, *o* or *u*.

Some words do not change at all, such as *Meerschweinchen*.

In a dictionary, the plural form is often shown in brackets:

der Hund(e) → Hunde
die Katze(n) → Katzen
der Vogel (¨) → Vögel

Words borrowed from another language usually add -*s*, as in English:

das Video → Videos

40 vierzig

2 Das ist meine Welt!

✏️ Schreiben

4 Mit einem Wörterbuch oder im Internet finde die Pluralform dieser Tiere.

Fisch   Pferd   Kaninchen   Panda   Ratte   Maus

5 Welche Tiere magst du? Welche Tiere magst du nicht? Schreib zwei Listen.

✓	✗
Ich mag Pandas.	Ich mag Ratten nicht.

ich mag — I like

⚙️ Strategie

Using sound-spelling links to work out meaning

If you do not immediately understand a word on the page, try saying it out loud:

eine Ratte
ein Kamel

What do you think they are?

🎧 Hören

6 🎵 Listen and answer the questions about two famous historical figures and their pets in English.

a What is each person's favourite animal?
b What other animal is mentioned?

🎭 Kultur

Mozart (top) was a very famous Austrian composer who wrote more than 600 works. He had a pet starling who could sing one of his melodies. E.T.A. Hoffmann (bottom) wrote the book that *The Nutcracker* is based on, as well as *The Sandman*. He loved his tomcat Kater Murr and devoted a whole book to him!

📖 Lesen

7 Read the comments about favourite animals. Copy and complete the table in English.

Name	Favourite animals	Further details
Elias	giraffes,	
Rita		

@Elias
Meine Lieblingstiere sind Giraffen und Elefanten. Giraffen sind so schlank und elegant.. :) :)

@Rita
Ich habe zwei Lieblingstiere: Walrosse und Delfine. Delfine sind sehr intelligent! 👍

@Bella
Ich habe viele Lieblingstiere: Wölfe, Bären, Elefanten. Ich mag auch Pinguine. ❤️ ❤️

@Kassim
Seehunde und Eisbären sind cool, aber meine Lieblingstiere sind Kamele und Orang-Utans. ❤️ ❤️ ❤️ ❤️ ❤️ ❤️ ❤️ Spektakulär! Aber Vögel mag ich gar nicht.

✏️ Schreiben

8 Was sind deine Lieblingstiere? Schreib einen kurzen Kommentar für das Forum aus Aktivität 7.

*Beispiel: Meine Lieblingstiere sind...
Sie sind...*

2 Kultur

Deutsche Kinder- und Jugendliteratur

📖 Lesen

1 Read the article. Are the statements true (T), false (F), or not in the text (NT)?

a Cornelia Funke is a world-famous children's author.
b Her breakthrough came in 2002 with *The Thief Lord*.
c Her *Ink World* trilogy followed *The Thief Lord*.
d Cornelia was an illustrator first and foremost.
e Cornelia loves animals.
f Cornelia lives on her own in California.

2 Schreib Cornelia Funkes Profil ab und füll es aus.

Cornelia Funke   Frosche, Hunde, Pferde   blau

10. Dezember   rot   ~~Oboe~~   blond

Autorin-Profil

Name: _____
Augenfarbe: _____
Haarfarbe: _____
Geburtstag: _____
Lieblingsfarbe: _____
Lieblingstiere: _____
Lieblingsmusikinstrument: Oboe

Cornelia Funke ist eine weltweit bekannte Autorin von Kinder- und Jugendliteratur.

Der internationale Durchbruch kam im Jahr 2002 mit *Herr der Diebe*. Dann kam *Drachenreiter* und die *Tintenwelt* Trilogie: *Tintenherz*, *Tintenblut* und *Tintentod*.

Cornelia Funke lebt mit ihrer Familie in Malibu, Kalifornien.

2 Das ist meine Welt!

✏️ Schreiben

3 Bring die Wörter in die richtige Reihenfolge.

Beispiel: heißt Wie du? → Wie heißt du?

a deine ist Was Lieblingsfarbe?
b Lieblingstiere? sind Was deine
c Lieblingsinstrument? dein ist Was
d du wohnst Wo?
e du Geburtstag? hast Wann
f deine Wie Haare? sind

🎧 Hören

4 Hör zu. Ist alles richtig?

🔄 Übersetzen

5 Translate the questions in activity 3 into English.

✏️ Schreiben

6 Schreib ein Interview mit Cornelia Funke.

Beispiel:
- Wie heißt du?
  Ich heiße Cornelia Funke.
- Was ist…?

📖 Lesen

7 Read the texts about Janosch's animal characters. Complete the sentences.

Hallo, ich bin der kleine Tiger.
Ich wohne mit meinem Freund Bär in einem Haus.

Hallo, ich bin die Tigerente.
Ich bin vierzig Jahre alt.
Ich habe am 15. März Geburtstag.
Ich bin das Spielzeug des Tigers im Buch, *Oh, wie schön ist Panama*.

Janosch is a very well-known children's illustrator and author. His real name is Horst Eckert and he was born on 11th March 1931. His successful children's books feature characters such as Little Bear, Little Tiger and the 'tiger duck'. His characters have appeared on many products – even on an aeroplane!

a Hello, I am the little _____ . I live with my _____ Little Bear in a _____ .

b Hello, I am the 'tiger duck'. I am _____ years old. My birthday is on 15th _____ . I am the _____ toy in the book, *The Trip to Panama*.

✏️ Schreiben

8 Schreib vier Sätze über Janosch. Beantworte folgende Fragen.

- Was ist sein richtiger (*real*) Name?
- Wann hat er Geburtstag?
- Wie sieht er aus?
- Was sind seine Lieblingstiere?

dreiundvierzig 43

2 Sprachlabor

Possessive adjectives

Possessive adjectives like 'my', 'your', 'his' and 'her' indicate to whom something belongs. In German, possessive adjectives take the same endings as the indefinite article *ein* and *kein*.

	m	f	n	pl
my	mein	mein**e**	mein	mein**e**
your	dein	dein**e**	dein	dein**e**
his	sein	sein**e**	sein	sein**e**
her	ihr	ihr**e**	ihr	ihr**e**

1 Complete the sentences with the correct form: *mein* or *meine* (a–c); *dein* or *deine* (d–f).

a _____ Schwester heißt Kaya.
b _____ Bruder ist acht Jahre alt.
c _____ Geschwister sind super!
d Wie heißt _____ Mutter?
e Wie heißen _____ Geschwister?
f Wie alt ist _____ Vater?

2 Write sentences about Leo's favourite things.

Example: **a** *Seine Lieblingsband ist Pur.*

a Lieblingsband (*f*): Pur
b Lieblingsstadt (*f*): Hamburg
c Lieblingssport (*m*): Tennis
d Lieblingsfarbe (*f*): blau
e Lieblingstiere (*pl*): Pinguine
f Lieblingsfußballer (*m*): Bastian Schweinsteiger
g Lieblingsessen (*n*): Pizza

Using the verb *haben*

In the sentence 'I have a brother.', 'I' is the subject who does the action (having), and 'brother' is a direct object (the thing that the subject has).

In German, the word for 'a' changes after the verb *haben* if the direct object that follows is masculine:

- *ein Bruder* → *Ich habe ein**en** Bruder.*

But it doesn't change when the object is feminine, neuter, or a plural:

- *eine Schwester* → *Ich habe eine Schwester.*
- *ein Haustier* → *Ich habe ein Haustier.*
- *keine Geschwister* → *Ich habe keine Geschwister.*

3 Match the beginning and ending of the sentences.

1 Ich heiße Prinz Heinrich und ich habe
2 Ich heiße Gretel und ich habe
3 Ich heiße Sebastian Vettel und ich habe einen
4 Ich heiße Rotkäppchen und ich habe
5 Ich heiße Aschenputtel und ich habe eine

a eine Oma.
b ein Schloss.
c einen Bruder.
d Ferrari.
e Stiefmutter.

4 Write sentences about what each person has.

Example: **a** *Karla hat ein Känguru.*

a Karla: Känguru (*n*)
b Gustav: Gorilla (*m*)
c Konrad: Krokodil (*n*)
d Gina: Giraffe (*f*)
e Dante: Delfin (*m*)
f Tanja: Tarantel (*f*)

2 Das ist meine Welt!

Plural nouns

In German, there are several ways of forming plural nouns.

Add -n, -en or -nen:

- die Schwester → die Schwester**n**
- die Lehrerin → die Lehrerin**nen**

Add -e:

- das Krokodil → die Krokodil**e**

Often words that gain -e in the plural also gain an umlaut, especially feminine words:

- die Maus → die M**äu**s**e**

Some words gain -er and an umlaut, or just an umlaut on the final a/o/u:

- der Mann → die M**än**n**er**
- der Bruder → die Br**ü**der

Some words don't change – for example, neuter nouns that end in -chen:

- das Mädchen → die Mädchen

Use a dictionary to find the correct ending in the plural – you will soon start to recognise patterns.

5 Put the letters in the correct order to write the plurals of the animals, family members or parts of the body.

a laSnchneg
b schiFe
c rerBüd
d netzKa
e rfePed
f nerwestSch
g Hndeä
h Beeni

6 Translate the sentences into German.

a I have three cats and four dogs.
b I have two horses and ten fish.
c I have three brothers and two sisters.
d I have two legs, two hands and two eyes.

Conjunctions *und*, *aber* and *oder*

Conjunctions allow you to link ideas and produce longer sentences. They show a higher level of language, and they help you sound more fluent and coherent.

und	and	used to add information
aber	but	used to show contrasting ideas
oder	or	used to offer alternatives

7 Translate the sentences into English.

a Ich habe einen Bruder und zwei Schwestern.
b Ich habe einen Bruder aber keine Schwester.
c Ich mag Hunde, aber ich mag Katzen nicht.
d Hast du einen Fisch oder einen Hund?
e Meine Mutter hat blonde Haare und blaue Augen.
f Findest du Fußball gut oder langweilig?

8 Complete the sentences with *und*, *aber* or *oder*.

a Ich habe schwarze Haare, _____ meine Schwester hat blonde Haare.
b Meine Lieblingsfarben sind blau _____ rot.
c Findest du Pop _____ Rap besser?
d Ich habe ein Pferd _____ einen Vogel.

Aussprache: -lich, -ig and -isch

Some common German adjective endings are -lich, -ig and -isch. Be careful with the 'ch' sound in -lich: it isn't the same as the 'ch' in 'church'. The ending -isch is pronounced 'ish'. (See p.111 for more practice of 'ch' and 'sch'.)

9 Listen and repeat. Then practise with your partner.

launisch   langweilig   praktisch
pummelig   dynamisch   freundlich
lustig   optimistisch

10 Practise saying the sentence.

Meine beste Freundin ist lustig – nicht langweilig oder launisch!

funfundvierzig

2 Was kann ich schon?

Lesen

1 Füll die Lücken mit den richtigen Wörtern aus.

Opa   Augen   Bruder   alt   Mutter
und   sechs   weiße   ist   lustig

Ich heiße Carlo und das ist meine Familie: Mein Vater heißt Luigi und meine **1** _____ heißt Maria. Ich habe einen **2** _____ und zwei Schwestern. Mein Bruder ist **3** _____ Jahre alt und sehr **4** _____ . Meine Schwestern sind ziemlich freundlich **5** _____ intelligent. Wir haben alle braune **6** _____ und schwarze Haare. Meine Oma und mein **7** _____ kommen aus Italien! Ich habe auch einen Hund. Mein Hund **8** _____ groß und treu. Er ist braun und hat **9** _____ Ohren. Mein Hund ist drei Jahre **10** _____ .

✓ 10

2 Read the text. Are the statements true (T) or false (F)?

Meine beste Freundin heißt Lara Lessmann. Sie hat am zehnten Februar Geburtstag und wohnt in Berlin. Sie hat lange blonde Haare und braune Augen. Sie ist sehr freundlich und kreativ. Sie ist schlank aber muskulös. Sie hat ein Nasenpiercing. Ihr Lieblingssport ist BMX-Rad fahren. Ihre Lieblingsfarbe ist weiß, aber ihr BMX-Rad ist schwarz. Sie hat auch eine grüne Schlange und einen Hund, Bello. Bello ist sehr treu.

a Her birthday is on 12th February.
b She has short blond hair.
c She has brown eyes.
d She is very friendly.
e She is tall and muscular.
f She has a pierced nose.
g Her favourite colour is white.
h Her bike is red.
i She has a dog and cat.
j Her dog is loyal.

✓ 10

Max. ✓ 20 Punkte

Hören

3 Listen to three people describing themselves or another person (1–3). Copy and complete the table in English. Sometimes there are two details to listen out for.

	1	2
Eye colour		
Hair colour/type		
Character		

✓ 10

4 Listen to the astronaut's call back to base. Answer the questions in English.

a What is the first name of the astronaut?
b What colour is the big alien?
c How many eyes does he have?
d How many arms and legs does he have?
e What is his stomach like?
f What colour is the small alien?
g What facial features does the alien have?
h How many arms does he have?
i What colour are his feet?
j Which alien has hair?

✓ 10

Max. ✓ 20 Punkte

2 Das ist meine Welt!

✏️ Schreiben

5 **Schreib Sätze mit diesen Wörtern.**

Beispiel: Du – keine Geschwister
Du hast keine Geschwister.

a Ich – kreativ
b Ich – blaue Augen
c Meine Lieblingsfarbe – gelb
d Mein Vater – Tom
e Mein Vater – 35

f Ich – Schwester
g Meine Schwester – blonde
h Meine Freundin – lustig
i habe – Hund
j Mein Hund – klein

✓ 10

6 **Übersetz die Sätze ins Deutsche.**

a I have a brother and a sister.
b My mum is intelligent and my dad is funny.
c I have a cat, but the cat is moody.
d My friend has green eyes and brown hair.
e Is your favourite colour blue or red?

✓ 10

Max. ✓ 20 Punkte

Deine Resultate

How many points did you get?

Ask your teacher for the answers. Write down your score out of a total of 20 for Reading. Then do the same for Listening and Writing.

Find the right combination of Bronze, Silver and Gold activities for you on pp.48–49!

Up to 6 points — Well done! Do the Bronze activity in the next section.

7–12 points — Great! Do the Silver activity in the next section.

13–20 points — Fantastic! Do the Gold activity in the next section.

2 Vorankommen!

Bronze

1 🎧 **Listen to six people talking about siblings. Copy and complete the table.**

	Brothers	Sisters
1	1	
2		
3		
4		
5		
6		

2 📖 **Read about the Troll family. Then answer the questions.**

Ich bin Talala Troll. Ich bin klein und blau. Ich habe eine große Nase und lange violette Haare. Meine Mutter ist rot und hat einen großen Bauch und große Ohren. Sie hat blaue Augen und blaue Haare. Mein Vater ist grün. Er hat einen großen Kopf und einen schwarzen Bart. Meine kleine Schwester Tululu Troll ist gelb. Sie hat lange weiße Haare und braune Augen.

Which family member:

a has blue hair?
b is yellow?
c has a big head?
d has a big nose?
e has big ears?
f has white hair?
g is green?
h has brown eyes?

3 ✏️ **Answer the questions in German.**

a Hast du Geschwister?
b Wie heißt dein Freund/deine Freundin?
c Wie siehst du aus?
d Was ist deine Lieblingsfarbe?
e Hast du ein Haustier?

Silber

4 🎧 **Listen. What can you see at the zoo? Complete the sentences in English.**

a There are _____ giraffes.
b There are _____ camels.
c There are twenty _____ .
d The highlight is a _____ .
e Mimi is very _____ .
f Hugo, the oldest animal, is a _____ .
g He is _____ years old.

5 📖 **Read the message and correct the statements.**

Hallo Simone,

heute schreibe ich dir über meine Familie. Ich habe einen Bruder und eine Schwester. Mein Bruder ist schon sechzehn Jahre alt. Ich finde meinen Bruder sehr cool. Meine Schwester ist neun Jahre alt. Sie hat lange schwarze Haare und ist ziemlich klein. Hast du ein Haustier? Wir haben drei große schwarze Fische, fünf kleine blaue Fische und einen braunen Fisch mit einem roten Kopf, aber ich finde die Fische langweilig.

Deine Eva

a Eva has two brothers.
b Her brother is 17 years old.
c She finds her sister cool.
d Her sister has long blond hair.
e One of Eva's fish has a yellow head.
f Eva finds the fish interesting.

6 ✏️ **Beschreib das Monster (40 Wörter). Gib folgende Informationen auf Deutsch.**
Describe the monster (40 words). Give the following information in German.

- what colour it is (*Es ist…*)
- its hair and eye colour (*Seine…*)
- another physical detail (*Es ist/hat…*)
- what personality it might have

2 Das ist meine Welt!

Gold

7 **Lies den Text über Hassans Großeltern. Wähl die richtige Antwort in den Sätzen unten.**

Meine Großeltern

Ich heiße Hassan. Meine Großeltern kommen aus der Türkei, aber sie wohnen seit 1972 in Deutschland.

Hier ist ein Foto aus dem Jahr 1970. Mein Opa, Islam, hat braune Haare und ist ziemlich muskulös. Er ist Fußballspieler. Meine Oma ist groß und schlank und hat lange schwarze Haare.

Heute ist meine Oma siebzig Jahre alt. Sie heißt Zehra. Sie ist ziemlich pummelig und sie hat mittellange weiße Haare und braune Augen. Sie ist sehr dynamisch und optimistisch.

Mein Opa ist dreiundsiebzig Jahre alt. Er hat kurze graue Haare, einen Schnurrbart und braune Augen. Er ist kreativ und oft lustig, aber er ist nicht mehr so fit. Seine Lieblingstiere sind Kaninchen.

Meine Großeltern sind die besten!

seit	since
heute	today, nowadays

a Hassan's grandparents live in **Turkey/Germany**.

b Hassan's grandparents both have **brown eyes/black hair**.

c There is an age difference between them of **three/five** years.

d Hassan's grandmother had **shorter/longer** hair in the 1970s.

e She is a very **positive/creative** person.

f Hassan thinks his grandfather is **funny/boring**.

g He is **sportier/less fit** nowadays.

h Hassan's grandfather has **a moustache/freckles**.

8 **Hör zu und lies nochmal den Text aus Aktivität 7. Finde acht Fehler (inkl. Beispiel).**

Beispiel: …sie wohnen seit ~~1972~~ 1975 in Deutschland.

9 **Schreib einen Text (60–80 Wörter) über eine Person in deiner Familie oder einen Freund/eine Freundin.**

Schreib:

- wie er/sie heißt
- wie alt er/sie ist
- wie er/sie aussieht
- etwas über seine/ihre Persönlichkeit
- etwas über seine/ihre Lieblingstiere und Haustiere.

🎁 Extra

You must use conjunctions (*und, aber* or *oder*) at least three times in your writing and you must include three intensifiers (*sehr, ziemlich, gar nicht, ein bisschen*).

neunundvierzig

2 Vokabeln

2.1 Bei mir zu Hause
At home

Hast du Geschwister?	*Do you have any brothers or sisters?*
Ich bin Einzelkind.	*I'm an only child.*
Ich habe einen Bruder/ eine Schwester.	*I have a brother/sister.*
Ich habe keine Geschwister.	*I have no brothers or sisters.*
der Bruder	brother
Eltern *(pl)*	parents
die Familie	family
Geschwister *(pl)*	siblings
Großeltern *(pl)*	grandparents
die Großmutter	grandmother
der Großvater	grandfather
der Halbbruder	half-brother
die Halbschwester	half-sister
die Mutter	mother
die Oma	grandmother
der Opa	grandfather
die Schwester	sister
der Stiefbruder	stepbrother
die Stiefmutter	stepmother
die Stiefschwester	stepsister
der Stiefvater	stepfather
der Vater	father
Zwillinge *(pl)*	twins
der Zwillingsbruder	twin brother
die Zwillingsschwester	twin sister
das Familienmodell	family model
die Patchworkfamilie	blended family
die Regenbogenfamilie	rainbow family
typisch	typical
zusammen leben	to live together

2.2 Wir sind Freunde
We are friends

Wie ist dein bester Freund/ deine beste Freundin?	*What's your best friend like?*
Er/Sie ist…	*He/She is…*
dynamisch	energetic
egoistisch	selfish
faul	lazy
frech	cheeky
freundlich	friendly
intelligent	intelligent
kreativ	creative
langweilig	boring
launisch	moody
lustig	funny
optimistisch	optimistic
respektvoll	respectful
schüchtern	shy
treu	loyal
auch	also
gar nicht	not at all
negativ	negative
positiv	positive
sehr	very
ziemlich	quite, fairly

2.3 Was ist deine Lieblingsfarbe?
What is your favourite colour?

die Farbe	colour
Meine Lieblingsfarbe ist…	*My favourite colour is…*
blau	blue
braun	brown
gelb	yellow

2 Das ist meine Welt!

grau	grey	groß	big, tall
grün	green	gut aussehend	good-looking
orange	orange	klein	small
rot	red	muskulös	muscular
schwarz	black	pummelig	chubby
violett	purple	schlank	thin
weiß	white		

aber	but
ein bisschen	a bit
nicht so	not very, not so
oder	or
und	and
vielleicht	perhaps

Wie siehst du aus?	What do you look like?
Wie sieht er/sie aus?	What does he/she look like?
Wie sind deine Augen?	What are your eyes like?
Wie sind deine Haare?	What is your hair like?

blond	blond
glatt	straight
kurz	short
lang	long
lockig	curly
mittellang	medium-length

2.5 Was sind deine Lieblingstiere?
What are you favourite animals?

Hast du ein Haustier?	Do you have a pet?
Ich habe kein Haustier.	I don't have a pet.

der Bart	beard
der Schnurrbart	moustache
Sommersprossen *(pl)*	freckles

2.4 Alles bunt!
Everything's colourful!

der Arm	arm	der Fisch	fish
der Bauch	stomach	der Hund	dog
das Bein	leg	der Kanarienvogel	canary
der Ellenbogen	elbow	das Kaninchen	rabbit
der Fuß	foot	die Katze	cat
das Gesicht	face	das Meerschweinchen	guinea pig
die Hand	hand	das Pferd	horse
das Knie	knee	die Schlange	snake
der Kopf	head	das Tier	animal
die Nase	nose	der Vogel	bird
Ohren *(pl)*	ears		
der Rücken	back	Ich mag/Ich mag (gar) nicht	I like/I don't like (at all)
die Schulter	shoulder		

einundfünfzig 51

3 Meine Freizeit
Los geht's!

1 In Deutschland, Österreich und der Schweiz gibt es so viele Wintersportarten *(types of winter sports)*! Was passt zusammen? Finde die Sportarten (1–8) im Bild (a–h).

1. Ski fahren
2. Snowboard fahren
3. Schlitten fahren
4. Schneeschuhwandern
5. Langlaufen
6. Eislaufen
7. Eisschwimmen
8. Eisangeln

2 Bring die Aktivitäten in die richtige Reihenfolge. Beginne mit Montag.

a. Am **Donnerstag** fahre ich Snowboard.
b. Ich fahre am **Samstag** Ski.
c. Am **Montag** gehen wir Eisschwimmen.
d. Am **Mittwoch** geht mein Bruder Eisangeln.
e. Meine Mutter geht am **Sonntag** Langlaufen.
f. Meine Freundin und ich gehen am **Dienstag** Schlitten fahren.
g. Geht ihr am **Freitag** Eislaufen?

3 Meine Freizeit

3 Welche Aktivitäten hat man vor 50 Jahren gemacht (*did people do 50 years ago*)? Welche Aktivitäten sind <u>nur</u> heute möglich (<u>only possible today</u>)? Schreib die Tabelle ab und füll sie aus.

ausruhen   Besuche machen   fernsehen   ins Internet gehen

~~mit dem Handy spielen~~   mit der Familie sein   Musik hören

Filme auf Netflix oder YouTube sehen   telefonieren

Theater/Konzerte besuchen

ausruhen	to relax
der Besuch	visit (noun)
fernsehen	to watch TV
besuchen	to visit (verb)

Vor 50 Jahren	Nur heute
	mit dem Handy spielen

4 Es ist das Jahr 1970. Was machst du in deiner Freizeit? Schreib eine Liste wie im Beispiel.

Beispiel: Montag – ausruhen, mit der Familie sein
Dienstag – …

5 Lies Steffi Grafs Profil und füll die Lücken aus.

Name: Steffi Graf

Geburtsort: Mannheim

Geburtstag: 14/6

Bekannt für: Tennis und Charity-Arbeit

Augenfarbe: blau

Haarfarbe: blond

Beginnt Tennis mit: drei Jahren

Grand-Slam-Titel in Tennis gewonnen: 22

a Steffi Graf hat blonde _____ und blaue _____ .
b Sie ist für _____ und Charity-Arbeit bekannt.
c Mit _____ Jahren beginnt sie, Tennis zu spielen.
d Sie hat _____ Grand-Slam-Titel gewonnen.
e Sie hat am _____ _____ Geburtstag.
f Sie ist in _____ geboren.

⚠ Achtung!

Sie hat … gewonnen and *Sie ist … geboren* describe events in the past. How would you translate them? You will learn more about talking about past events and using different tenses in later units.

3.1 Sport macht Spaß!

Objectives
- Talking about sport
- Revising the present tense
- Manipulating language

Willi der Wunderhund

📖 Lesen

1 Was passt zusammen? Verbinde die Sätze (1–8) mit den Bildern (a–h).

Welche Sportarten machst du, Willi?

1. Ich mache Yoga.
2. Ich mache Judo und Karate.
3. Ich gehe ins Fitnesscenter und ich jogge.
4. Ich spiele Tennis und Federball.
5. Ich spiele Rugby und Fußball.
6. Ich gehe schwimmen. Ich gehe auch angeln.
7. Ich tanze Ballett.
8. Ich spiele Basketball.

a b c  d 
e f g  h

🎧 Hören

2 Hör zu. Ist alles richtig?

3 Hör zu. Welche Sportarten aus Aktivität 1 (a–h) macht Willis Schwester, Wilhelmina die Wunderhündin (1–8)?

Beispiel: **1** g

Aussprache

Remember that in German, 'w' is pronounced as 'v'. Practise saying this sentence:

Willi und Waldemar wandern am Wochenende im Wald. (Willi and Waldemar go walking in the woods at the weekend.)

⚙ Strategie

Manipulating language

Once you know the correct verb endings in German, you can build phrases applying to anyone you choose (*du, sie, wir*, etc.). You already use different verb endings in English ('I play' → 'he play**s**') – it will start to feel natural in German, too.

✏ Schreiben

4 Schreib acht Sätze für Wilhelmina.

Beispiel: **1** *Wilhelmina macht Judo und Karate.*

3 Meine Freizeit

💬 Sprechen

5 👥 **Du bist Willi oder Wilhelmina. Du machst eine Sportart. Dein Partner/Deine Partnerin muss raten (*has to guess*), was das ist.**

Beispiel:
- *Welche Sportart machst du heute, Willi?*
- *(Mime your sport.)*
- *Machst du Yoga?*
- *Nein, ich tanze Ballett./Ja, ich mache Yoga.*

Aa Grammatik
p.67; WB p.29

The present tense of regular verbs

The verb *spielen* is regular. To form the present tense, remember to take the stem (*spiel-*) and add these endings:

ich spiel**e**
du spiel**st**
er/sie/es spiel**t**
wir spiel**en**
ihr spiel**t**
sie/Sie spiel**en**

You can do the same for *machen* (to do or make), *gehen* (to go) or *Sport treiben* (to do sport).

🎧 Hören

6 〰️ **Listen to five people giving their opinions of sports. Copy and complete the table in English. Write all of the information you hear.**

Name	Sport	Opinion
1 Lisa-Marie	basketball	fun
2 Abdul		
3 Marcus		
4 Malek		
5 Lara		

Es gefällt mir.	I like it.
Es macht Spaß.	It's fun./It's great.
Es ist toll.	It's great.
Es ist entspannend.	It's relaxing.
Es gefällt mir nicht.	I don't like it.
Es ist langweilig.	It's boring.
Es ist schwierig.	It's difficult.
Es ist anstrengend.	It's exhausting.

💬 Sprechen

7 👥 **Macht sechs Dialoge.**

Beispiel:
- *Wie findest du Gymnastik?*
- *Es gefällt mir. Es macht Spaß.*

🔄 Übersetzen

8 **Übersetz Fatimas Blogeintrag ins Deutsche.**

Hi! How are you? I'm Fatima and I'm 15. Sport is great, but I don't go to the gym! I play football. It's tiring, but it's fun. I also do yoga. It's relaxing. And you?

fünfundfünfzig

3.2 Das mache ich gern!

Objectives
- Talking about your hobbies
- Using irregular verbs
- Asking questions

📖 Lesen

1 Lies die Umfrage (*survey*). Verbinde die Fragen (1–12) mit den Bildern (a–l).

Was machst du in deiner Freizeit?

1. Spielst du gern Videospiele?
2. Machst du gern Musik?
3. Chattest du gern mit Freunden?
4. Faulenzst du gern?
5. Gehst du gern ins Kino?
6. Malst oder bastelst du gern?
7. Hörst du gern Musik?
8. Gehst du gern einkaufen?
9. Liest du gern?
10. Fährst du gern Rad?
11. Fährst du gern Skateboard?
12. Siehst du gern fern?

🎧 Hören

2 Hör zu. Was macht Jana gern (1–12)? Schreib die Tabelle ab und füll sie mit den Hobbys aus Aktivität 1 (a–l) aus.

Sehr gern ✓✓	Gern ✓	Gar nicht gern ✗
d, …		

💬 Sprechen

3 👥 Macht die Umfrage aus Aktivität 1.

> Was machst du in deiner Freizeit? Spielst du gern Videospiele?

> Ja, ich spiele sehr gern Videospiele.

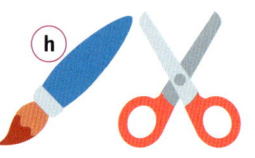

Sprachmuster

The word *gern* is very common in German. It translates roughly as 'eagerly' or 'with pleasure'. Add it straight after the verb, or after *nicht* in a negative sentence, to say whether or not you like or enjoy doing something.

Ich tanze. (I dance.)
*Ich tanze **gern**.* (I like dancing.)
*Sie tanzt nicht **gern**.* (She doesn't like dancing.)

Grammatik p.66; WB p.31

The present tense of irregular verbs

You learnt the regular verbs *machen* and *spielen* earlier in Unit 3. The verbs *fahren*, *sehen* and *lesen* are irregular. These verbs take the same present tense endings as regular verbs, but have vowel changes in the *du* and *er/sie/es* forms:

fahren	**sehen**	**lesen**
ich fahre	ich sehe	ich lese
du f**ä**hrst	du s**ie**hst	du l**ie**st
er/sie/es f**ä**hrt	er/sie/es s**ie**ht	er/sie/es l**ie**st

*S**ie**hst du gern fern? Ja, ich sehe sehr gern fern.*

56 sechsundfünfzig

3 Meine Freizeit

Thomas

Hallo!
Ich heiße Thomas.
Ich wohne in Jena. Jena gefällt mir. Jena ist eine tolle und attraktive Stadt. Ich bin 14 Jahre alt und ich bin ziemlich aktiv. Ich tanze sehr gern. Ich tanze Hip-Hop und ich tanze auch Ballett. Ich finde es anstrengend, aber es macht Spaß! Ich höre sehr gern Musik und ich chatte auch gern mit Freunden. Ich gehe nicht gern einkaufen. Ich finde es so langweilig!

Amela

Grüß dich!
Ich heiße Amela und ich wohne in Igls in Österreich. Das schreibt man I-G-L-S. Das ist ein Dorf – klein aber perfekt! Im Winter kann man Ski und Snowboard fahren, alles! Für mich ist aktiv sein sehr positiv. Ich bin dynamisch und ziemlich sportlich und ich fahre sehr gern Rad. So COOL! Es ist schwierig aber spannend.
Ich sehe gar nicht gern fern. Sport ist besser!

Lesen

4 Read Thomas and Amela's profiles and answer Thomas (T) or Amela (A).

a Who likes dance?
b Who lives in a village?
c Who likes sport?
d Who doesn't like watching TV?
e Who doesn't like shopping?

5 Finde die passenden Sätze (a–f) in den Profilen von Thomas und Amela.

a I like dancing very much.
b I find it tiring, but it's fun!
c I don't like going shopping.
d I am energetic and fairly sporty.
e It's difficult but exciting.
f I don't like watching TV at all.

Übersetzen

6 Übersetz die Sätze ins Deutsche.

a I like playing music.
b Do you (du) like chatting with friends?
c She likes listening to music.
d We don't like dancing.
e They like playing football very much.

Strategie

Asking questions

The key to asking questions with a 'yes' or 'no' answer in German is to swap round the subject and the verb:

Hört er gern Musik? Ja, er **hört** gern Musik.

Can you think of any questions in English that are formed in this way?

Schreiben

7 Was machst du in deiner Freizeit? Schreib dein Profil.

Ich heiße ... und ich wohne in...			
Ich	spiele	gern	Videospiele/Musik.
	sehe		fern.
	chatte	sehr gern	mit Freunden.
	fahre	gar nicht gern	Skateboard/Rad.
	höre/mache		Musik.
	lese/male/bastele	gern/sehr gern/gar nicht gern.	
	finde es	toll/entspannend/langweilig.	

Extra

Write a profile for your partner, using *er* or *sie* verb forms. Use your partner's survey answers from activity 3.

3.3 Hast du Zeit?

Objectives
- Saying how often you do something
- Applying the 'verb-second' rule
- Tackling longer reading passages

📖 Lesen

1 Read the article on how young people in Germany spend their free time. Complete the sentences in English.

Freizeitumfrage

Wie verbringen Jugendliche in Deutschland ihre Zeit?

An erster Stelle kommt die Schule. Ab 13 Jahre arbeiten Jugendliche 44 Stunden pro Woche in der oder für die Schule. Wow!

An zweiter Stelle verbringen Jugendliche Zeit mit ihrer Familie.

An dritter Stelle finden wir chillen (ausruhen, faulenzen, Musik hören, lesen, basteln oder malen) mit 15 Wochenstunden.

Auf Platz vier mit 14 Stunden kommen zocken und fernsehen.

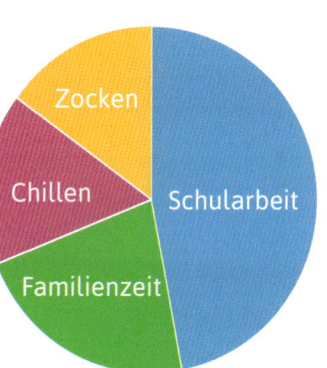

Pie chart: Zocken, Chillen, Familienzeit, Schularbeit

verbringen	to spend (time)
an erster/zweiter/dritter Stelle	in first/second/third place
zocken	to game, to play video games

a From the age of _____ , young people spend _____ hours per week working in or for school.
b After schoolwork, young people spend time with _____ .
c Young people spend _____ hours per week doing relaxing activities.
d Fourteen hours per week are spent on _____ and _____ .

🎧 Hören

2 Listen to Zelma talking about what she does in her free time. How often does she do each activity? Make notes in English.

Example: **a** now and then

a gaming
b cinema
c chatting with friends
d painting
e crafting

oft	often	selten	rarely
manchmal	sometimes	nie	never
ab und zu	now and then		

Grammatik p.66; WB p.33

The 'verb-second' rule

In German, the main verb comes as the second idea in a sentence. It might not be the second word!

1st idea	2nd idea	Remaining idea
Die Schule	**kommt**	an erster Stelle.
An erster Stelle	**kommt**	die Schule.
Ich	**spiele**	oft Fußball.
Oft	**spiele**	ich Fußball.

💬 Sprechen

3 „Was machst du oft? Was machst du nie?" Macht Dialoge.

🎁 Extra

Justify your answers in activity 3 using *denn* ('because'):
Ich lese oft, denn ich finde es entspannend.

3 Meine Freizeit

Lesen

4 🎵 Hör zu und lies.

Dzsenifer Marozsán, Fußballstar

1 Dzsenifer Marozsán ist eine deutsche Fußballspielerin. Sie spielt für Olympique Lyonnais. Sie hat am 18. April Geburtstag.

2 Im Alter von drei Jahren spielt Dzsenifer Marozsán Klavier aber nicht sehr gern. Es gefällt ihr gar nicht. Sie spielt lieber Fußball. Fußball macht Spaß!

3 Dzsenifers Familie kommt aus Ungarn. Als Kind trainiert sie jeden Tag mit ihrem Vater. Ihr Vater heißt Janos. Ihre Mutter heißt Erika. Dzsenifer hat einen Bruder, David. Er spielt auch Fußball.

4 Dzsenifer hat lange braune Haare und braune Augen. Sie ist sehr optimistisch aber ein bisschen schüchtern. Dzsenifer hat viele Tattoos: die Geburtsdaten ihrer Großeltern und auch ein Porträt ihrer Eltern.

5 Dzsenifer ist die bisher jüngste Bundesliga-Spielerin aller Zeiten! Sie spielt zum ersten Mal im Alter von 14 Jahren in der Bundesliga.

6 Dzsenifer ist für ihre Tricks bekannt. Täglich übt sie ihre Tricks! Jeden Tag macht sie Fitness und trainiert. Jeden Abend faulenzt sie. Sie chillt!

7 Einmal pro Woche spielt sie mit ihrer Mannschaft. Und am Wochenende spielt sie Videospiele. Das findet sie toll.

das Klavier	piano	üben	to practise
Sie spielt lieber Fußball.	She prefers to play football.	einmal pro Woche	once a week
als Kind	as a child	die Mannschaft	team

5 Verbinde die Paragrafen (1–7) aus Aktivität 4 mit den Titeln (a–g).

a Dzsenifers Familie
b Ein typischer Tag für Dszenifer
c Dzsenifers Woche
d Dzsenifers Liebe zu Fußball
e Dzsenifers Aussehen und Persönlichkeit
f Fakten über Dszenifer
g Dzsenifer und die Bundesliga

6 Read the text again. Answer the questions in English.

a Give two details about Dzsenifer's brother.
b What sort of a person is Dzsenifer?
c Describe one of Dzsenifer's tattoos.
d How old was Dzsenifer when she first played for the *Bundesliga*?
e What is she known for?
f What does she do at the weekend?

Strategie

Tackling longer reading passages

- Don't be put off by the length of a passage. With the passage in activity 4, you have already seen 90% of the content.
- You don't have to understand every single word to make sense of it.
- Try to use context to help you with an unfamiliar word. What would you expect it to mean?
- Your knowledge of grammar and word patterns will help you. Where will the main verb in a sentence appear? Could a very long word just be a compound noun that you can easily break down?

Übersetzen

7 Translate the final paragraph of *Dzsenifer Marozsán, Fußballstar* into English.

neunundfünfzig 59

3.4 Was für Musik hörst du gern?

Objectives
- Talking about music you listen to and play
- Using (gar nicht) gern, lieber, am liebsten
- Talking about things you haven't experienced

🎧 Hören

1 Hör zu. Welchen Radiosender (*radio station*) hören sie (1–6)?

Beispiel: **1** *Nummer Eins*

🎭 Kultur

Schlager is a very popular music genre in Germany, combining folk, pop and sugary, romantic lyrics. Helene Fischer is one of its most famous stars.

Was kommt im Radio?

Klassik Live: klassische Musik

Radio You: Popmusik

Schlagermix Pur: Schlager-Hits aus Deutschland

Nummer Eins: Hip-Hop und Deutschrap

Kult-Rock.de: Indie und Rockmusik

Rainbow FM: elektronische Musik und Techno

📖 Lesen

2 Read the opinions. Copy and complete the table in English.

> @lia
> Ich höre gar nicht gern Rock. Es gefällt mir gar nicht. Ich höre gern Pop. Ich höre lieber Hip-Hop, aber am liebsten höre ich Techno. Ich tanze gern.
>
> @arman
> Ich höre gar nicht gern Deutschrap. Es gefällt mir nicht. Es ist hart und aggressiv. Ich höre gern klassische Musik. Ich höre lieber Schlager aber am liebsten Pop. Ich mag die Melodien.

	Lia	Arman
Dislikes	rock	
Likes		
Prefers		
Likes best		

🎧 Hören

3 Hör zu. Notiere die Musikart und die Meinung (*opinion*) (1–3): gar nicht gern, gern, lieber, am liebsten.

Beispiel: **1** *Schlager: gar nicht gern, Techno:…*

Aa Grammatik   p.67; WB p.35

Using (*gar nicht*) *gern*, *lieber*, *am liebsten*

You have already encountered *gern* and *gar nicht gern*. To say what you prefer, use *lieber*. *Am liebsten* is used to say what you like best of all.

gar nicht gern	Ich spiele **gar nicht gern** Fußball.
gern	Ich spiele **gern** Korbball.
lieber	Ich spiele **lieber** Rugby.
am liebsten	Ich spiele **am liebsten** Tennis.

Remember the 'verb-second' rule:
<u>Ich</u> **spiele** am liebsten Tennis.   Am liebsten **spiele** <u>ich</u> Tennis.

3 Meine Freizeit

📖 Lesen

4 Lies die Meinungen und finde die passenden Ausdrücke (a–h) auf Deutsch.

Beispiel: **a** *ein berühmter Komponist*

a a famous composer
b symphonies
c I find his voice beautiful.
d songs
e The lyrics are very inspiring.
f my favourite (female) singer
g she sings
h I find his beats great.

> Ludwig van Beethoven ist ein berühmter Komponist. Er komponierte viele Symphonien, aber mein Lieblingsstück heißt *Für Elise*. Ich kann das auf dem Klavier spielen.

> Xavier Naidoo ist mein Lieblingssänger und ich finde seine Stimme schön. Er hat viele tolle R&B-Lieder geschrieben und die Liedtexte sind sehr inspirierend.

> Meine Lieblingssängerin heißt Helene Fischer. Sie singt deutsche Schlager und sie hat Hunderttausende von Fans. Ich finde ihre Musik super!

> Ich liebe Rap-Musik, aber ich finde deutschen Rap besser als englischen Rap. Mein Lieblingsrapper ist Samy Deluxe. Ich finde seine Beats genial.

5 Was passt zusammen?

Beispiel: **1** c

Ich spiele...
1 Gitarre.
2 Schlagzeug.
3 Trompete.
4 Geige.
5 Klavier.

🎧 Hören

6 Hör zu. Ist alles richtig?

💬 Sprechen

7 Macht Dialoge.

Was für Musik hörst du (nicht) gern?	Ich höre (nicht) gern/lieber/am liebsten…
Warum?	Es gefällt mir (gar nicht). Ich mag die Melodien/die Beats/ die coolen Texte. Es ist inspirierend/hart/aggressiv.
Spielst du ein Instrument?	Ja, ich spiele… Nein, ich bin nicht musikalisch, aber…

⚙ Strategie

Talking about things you haven't experienced

When learning languages, you may be asked to speak or write about things (holidays, sports, hobbies, family events) you haven't experienced yourself, such as *Spielst du ein Instrument?* Don't panic if your answer is *nein!* You can also:

- explain why you don't do something: *Ich bin nicht musikalisch.*
- say whether you'd like to do something: *Ich möchte* ('I would like to') *Klavier spielen.*
- say what you do instead: *Ich höre lieber Rap.*

✏ Schreiben

8 Schreib einen kurzen Text über deine Lieblingsmusik. Du kannst deine Antworten aus Aktivität 7 aufschreiben.

einundsechzig

3.5 Stars und Trends – was gibt's Neues?

Objectives
- Talking about famous people and online life
- Starting to recognise different tenses
- Extending your writing

Lesen

1 Hör zu und lies.

Sein Name ist Bam. Julien Bam!

Julien Bam ist ein deutscher Webvideoproduzent. Er macht Videos über Fotografie, Tanzen, Musik und Lifestyle. Er hat mehr als fünf Millionen Follower und Abonnenten.

Julien ist in Aachen geboren, aber er hat auch in Singapur und Köln gewohnt. Seine drei Lieblingsorte sind Aachen, Singapur und Köln. Er ist 31 Jahre alt und hat am 23. November Geburtstag.

Er ist für seine Kurzfilme und Musikvideos sehr bekannt, vor allem sein Video *Most Epic Dance Moves*. Julien Bam ist berühmt, sehr populär und sehr beliebt, denn er ist dynamisch, sehr positiv, lustig und freundlich.

Als Kind wollte Julien Astronaut werden. Möchtest du lieber Astronaut oder Webvideoproduzent werden?

der Webvideoproduzent	online video producer, vlogger
Abonnenten (pl)	subscribers
Möchtest du … werden?	Would you like to become…?

2 Read the text again. Copy and complete the fact file about Julien Bam in English.

- Name: _____
- Job: _____
- Number of followers/subscribers: _____
- Birthplace: _____
- Favourite places: _____
- Age: _____
- Characteristics: _____
- Childhood ambition: _____

Grammatik — WB p.37

Starting to recognise different tenses

You have learnt how to recognise and use the present tense. The text in activity 1 also uses tenses that relate to past events:

Er **hat** in Singapur **gewohnt**.
(He **lived** in Singapore. – perfect tense)

Er **wollte** Astronaut **werden**.
(He **wanted to become** an astronaut. – imperfect tense)

At this stage, you can use context and time markers (e.g. *als Kind…*) to work out meaning.

Sprechen

3 Macht ein Interview mit Julien Bam.

- Wie heißt du?
- Wie viele Abonnenten hast du?
- Wofür bist du bekannt?
- Was machst du gern?
- Wie alt bist du?
- Wann hast du Geburtstag?
- Beschreib dich!

3 Meine Freizeit

✏️ Schreiben

4 Schreib einen Artikel über Lisa und Lena. Benutz den Text aus Aktivität 1 zur Hilfe (*for help*).

Namen: Lisa und Lena
Beruf: Webvideoproduzentinnen, Influencer
Fans/Abonnenten: 15,2 Millionen
Geburtsort: Stuttgart
Haarfarbe: blond
Augenfarbe: braun
Alter: 18
Bekannt für: Videos, Tanzen und Playback singen
Charakter: cool, kreativ, energisch, nett

Die Zwillinge „LeLi"

🎧 Hören

5 Du hörst Dialoge (1–9) über soziale Medien. Welche Frage hörst du (a–i)?

Beispiel: **1** c

a   Hast du ein Handy?
b   Hast du einen Computer?
c   Hast du ein Online-Profil?
d   Wie oft bist du online?
e   Machst du gern Selfies?
f   Wie oft likst du Fotos?
g   Teilst du oft Bilder?
h   Siehst du gern Videoclips?
i   Wie oft hörst du Musik online?

Teilst du…?   Do you share…?

⚙️ Strategie

Extending your writing

Don't panic when asked to write longer texts in German. Break it down into stages.

Plan what to say using the vocab and grammar you've learnt. Can you use an existing text as a model?

Keep it simple but write as much as you can, adding reasons and detail where possible.

Finally, check your spelling and review your grammar: genders, verb endings, word order.

⚠️ Achtung!

You can describe just Lisa <u>or</u> Lena in activity 4 (*sie hat, sie ist, …*). To write about both sisters as a duo, remember to use the third person plural ('they') form of the verb: (*sie haben, sie sind, …*).

🔄 Übersetzen

6 Translate the questions from activity 5 into English.

💬 Sprechen

7 👥 Macht ein Interview über soziale Medien. Partner A stellt fünf Fragen aus Aktivität 5 und Partner B antwortet. Dann tauscht die Rollen (*swap roles*).

✏️ Schreiben

8 Schreib deine Antworten aus Aktivität 7 auf.

Aussprache

Many German words relating to technology are borrowed from English, but do they sound the same? Listen again to the words *Handy*, *Computer*, *Fotos*, *Profil* and *online* in activity 5 and practise 'Germanising' your pronunciation of technology terms in your interview in activity 7.

3 Kultur

Ich male gern!

Hören

1 Hör zu. Welches Bild ist das (1–3)?

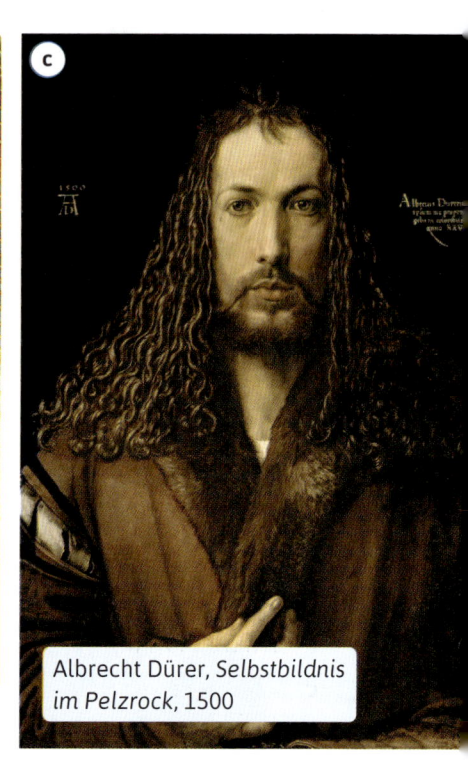

a) Paul Klee, *Der Goldfisch*, 1925

b) Hundertwasser, *Der Europäer Der Sich Seinen Schnurbart Hält*, 1951

c) Albrecht Dürer, *Selbstbildnis im Pelzrock*, 1500

Sprechen

2 Macht drei Dialoge.

Was siehst du auf dem Bild?	Auf dem Bild sehe ich	einen Mann. eine Frau.	Er hat... Sie hat...
Wie findest du das Bild?	Ich finde das Bild interessant/toll/kindlich/langweilig. Es gefällt mir. Ich mag die Farben/die coolen Formen. Es ist inspirierend. Es gefällt mir gar nicht. Es ist hart/aggressiv. Es ist sehr altmodisch/modern/kindlich.		

Paul Klee was born in Switzerland. A playful artist, with a childlike perspective, Klee often used musical notation in his work.

Hundertwasser (Friedrich Stowasser) was an Austrian artist who loved spirals and colour.

Albrecht Dürer was a painter and printmaker who created the first known self-portrait, aged just 13. He was inspired by travelling in Italy.

3 Meine Freizeit

📖 Lesen

3 Read the text and answer the questions in English.

Das Duo Herakut

Sie heißt Jasmin Siddiqui (Hera) und er heißt Falk Lehmann (Akut). Zusammen sind sie *Herakut*.

Sie lernten sich in 2004 bei einem Festival in Spanien kennen.

Ihr Projekt heißt *Giant Storybook*. Zwei Kinder, zwei Riesen, zwei Welten. Viele Wände. Das Kinderbuch existiert auf Papier, die Bilder findet man überall.

Ihre Bilder sind inspirierend. Was meinst du?

zusammen	together
sie lernten sich kennen	they got to know each other
zwei Riesen	two giants
viele Wände	many walls
überall	all over (everywhere)

a What are the artists' names?
b Where did they meet?
c How many worlds does the 'Giant Storybook' have?
d Where can you find the children's book?
e Where are the illustrations?

✏️ Schreiben

4 Beschreib dieses Bild vom *Giant Storybook*. Gib deine Meinung. (*Give your opinion.*)

Auf der Wand sehe ich	Kinder. Tiere. Bücher. Buchstaben. Bäume.

Ich finde das Bild…
Ich mag…
Es ist…
…gefällt mir (nicht).

3 Sprachlabor

The present tense of irregular verbs

Irregular verbs such as *fahren*, *sehen* and *lesen* take the same present tense endings as regular verbs, but have vowel changes in the stem for the *du* and *er/sie/es* forms.

Infinitive verb	Stem	Stem vowel change for *du* and *er/sie/es* forms
fahren	fahr-	fähr-
sehen	seh-	sieh-
lesen	les-	lies-

1 Complete the sentences with the correct form of *fahren*.

a Meine Schwester _____ Snowboard.
b Ich _____ Ski.
c Meine Eltern _____ Rad.
d _____ du Ski?
e Wir _____ Skateboard.
f _____ ihr Skateboard?

2 Match the beginning and ending of the sentences.

1 Ich sehe
2 Meine Mutter
3 Meine Geschwister
4 Siehst
5 Wir fahren
6 Ihr

a fahren Snowboard.
b gern fern.
c fahrt sehr gut Ski!
d du gern Disney-Filme?
e Rad.
f sieht nicht gern fern.

Applying the 'verb-second' rule

The main verb is always the second idea in a sentence. This does not necessarily mean the second word! When a sentence starts with a time or frequency expression ('sometimes', 'at the weekend', etc.), you swap round the verb and the subject (*ich*, *du*, etc.) that comes after the expression, so that the verb stays in second position. This is called 'inversion'.

- Ich **spiele** Fußball.
- Am Wochenende ~~ich spiele~~ **spiele** ich Fußball.

3 Put the words in the correct order. Start each sentence with the word in bold.

a höre ich **Jeden** Musik Tag.
b Bruder malt **Nie** mein.
c **Oft** wir einkaufen gehen.
d Skateboard und ich fahre **Ab** zu.
e **Manchmal** Internet surft Alex im.
f ich Freunden mit chatte **Täglich**.

4 Translate the sentences into German.

a On Tuesday I do yoga.
b On Wednesday I go swimming.
c On Thursday I listen to music.
d On Friday I play video games.
e On Saturday I go shopping.
f On Sunday I go to the cinema.
g I never watch TV.
h Sometimes I play basketball.

3 Meine Freizeit

Using (gar nicht) gern, lieber, am liebsten

To say that you like doing something, you use *gern* straight after the verb. Depending on the degree of how much you like or dislike something, you can use:

(gar) nicht gern	indicates 'dislike'
gern	indicates 'like'
lieber	indicates 'prefer'
am liebsten	indicates 'like best of all'

Notice that, unlike in English, the sentences still use the same main verb rather than 'to like' or 'to prefer'. The words *gern*, *lieber* and *am liebsten* modify the meaning:

- *Ich lese gern.*
  (I like reading.)
- *Ich höre lieber Musik.*
  (I prefer listening to music.)
- *Am liebsten male ich.*
  (I like painting best of all.)

5 Match the beginning and ending of the sentences. Then translate the sentences into English.

1. Ich spiele nicht gern
2. Meine Schwester geht lieber
3. Wir hören am liebsten
4. Anja und Niklas, ihr fahrt gern
5. Du siehst nicht gern

a Tennis.   b einkaufen.   c fern.
d Rap.   e Ski.

6 Translate the sentences into German.

a I like playing video games.
b Jan doesn't like listening to music.
c Maya prefers to go shopping.
d I like to go snowboarding best of all.
e Do you (*du*) like reading?

The present tense of regular verbs

To form the present tense of regular verbs such as *spielen* and *machen*, take the stem of the verb and add the following endings:

*ich spiel**e***
*du spiel**st***
*er/sie/es spiel**t***
*wir spiel**en***
*ihr spiel**t***
*sie/Sie spiel**en***

It helps to think of familiar phrases when in doubt, e.g. *Ich hab-**e** einen Bruder. Ich wohn-**e** in Berlin. Wo wohn-**st** du? Meine Mutter ha-**t** lange Haare.*

7 Add the correct endings to the verb stems.

a Mein Bruder spiel___ Tennis.
b Ich treib___ nicht viel Sport.
c Bruno und Gitte geh___ ins Fitnesscenter.
d Wir tanz___ gern.
e Treib___ du Sport?
f Geh___ ihr gern schwimmen?
g Sergio mach___ Judo.
h Mein Vater und ich geh___ angeln.

Aussprache: v and w

In German, the letter 'v' usually sounds like 'f,' but in some words which are of foreign origin (such as the name *Vanessa*), the letter is pronounced like the English 'v'. The German letter 'w' sounds like the English letter 'v'.

8 **Listen and repeat. Then practise with your partner.**

Vater   Woche   vier
Winter   November   Wort
Wort   Volkswagen   wohnen

9 **Practise saying the tongue twister.**

Wo wohnen Volker und Vanessa? Volker und Vanessa wohnen in Wien.

siebenundsechzig

3 Was kann ich schon?

📖 Lesen

1 Was passt zusammen? Verbinde die Fragen (1–10) mit den Antworten (a–j).

1. Treibst du Sport?
2. Wie oft bist du online?
3. Tanzt du gern?
4. Spielst du ein Instrument?
5. Was hörst du im Radio?
6. Welche Musik gefällt dir nicht?
7. Wer ist dein Lieblingssänger?
8. Hast du ein Handy?
9. Was machst du im Internet?
10. Was machst du in deiner Freizeit?

a. Nein, ich finde Tanzen langweilig.
b. Ich höre gern Popmusik.
c. Ja, ich habe ein Handy.
d. Ja, ich spiele Fußball.
e. Ich schaue Videoclips.
f. Ja, ich spiele Gitarre.
g. Mein Lieblingssänger ist Ed Sheeran.
h. Ich mache Judo und lese gern.
i. Klassische Musik gefällt mir nicht.
j. Ich bin jeden Tag online.

✓ 10

2 Read the text. Copy and complete the profile in English.

> Sie heißt Anna Katharina Schaffelhuber und kommt aus Regensburg in Deutschland. Sie liebt Sport und ihr Lieblingssport ist Ski fahren. 2014 hat sie in den Paralympischen Winterspielen fünf Goldmedaillen gewonnen. Das war super! In ihrer Freizeit liest sie gern und verbringt Zeit mit ihrer Familie.
>
> An der Universität studiert sie Mathematik. Sie ist oft online: Sie teilt Fotos und chattet mit ihren Freunden. Sie hat ein Online-Profil bei Facebook und sie möchte Teenager inspirieren, Sport zu treiben, auch wenn es schwierig ist.

a. Name: _____
b. Nationality: _____
c. Favourite sport: _____
d. Number of gold medals in 2014: _____
e. Free-time activities: (2 marks) _____
f. Studies: _____
g. Online activities: (2 marks) _____
h. Her goal: _____

✓ 10

Max. ✓ 20 Punkte

🎧 Hören

3 〰️ Listen and write the activities Malia has planned for Monday to Sunday in English. Some days have two activities.

✓ 10

4 〰️ Listen to the results of a survey on how young people spend their free time. Complete the sentences in English.

a. _____ percent of teenagers play sport.
b. The sport they like most is _____ .
c. Ninety percent of teenagers like to _____ .
d. They also like to _____ and _____ . (**two** hobbies)
e. Their favourite type of music is _____ .
f. The type of music they dislike is _____ .
g. Many find playing an instrument relaxing, but some find it _____ .
h. _____ percent of young people have a mobile phone.
i. They spend two hours a day _____ .

✓ 10

Max. ✓ 20 Punkte

68 achtundsechzig

3 Meine Freizeit

✏️ Schreiben

5 In jedem Satz fehlt ein Wort. (*A word is missing in each sentence.*) Korrigiere die Sätze.

a Ich gern Tennis.
b Meine Lieblingsmusik Pop.
c Spielst ein Instrument?
d Jeden Tag höre Musik.
e Susi gern Rad.

✓ 5

6 Was machen sie (nicht) gern? Schreib einen Satz über jede Person.

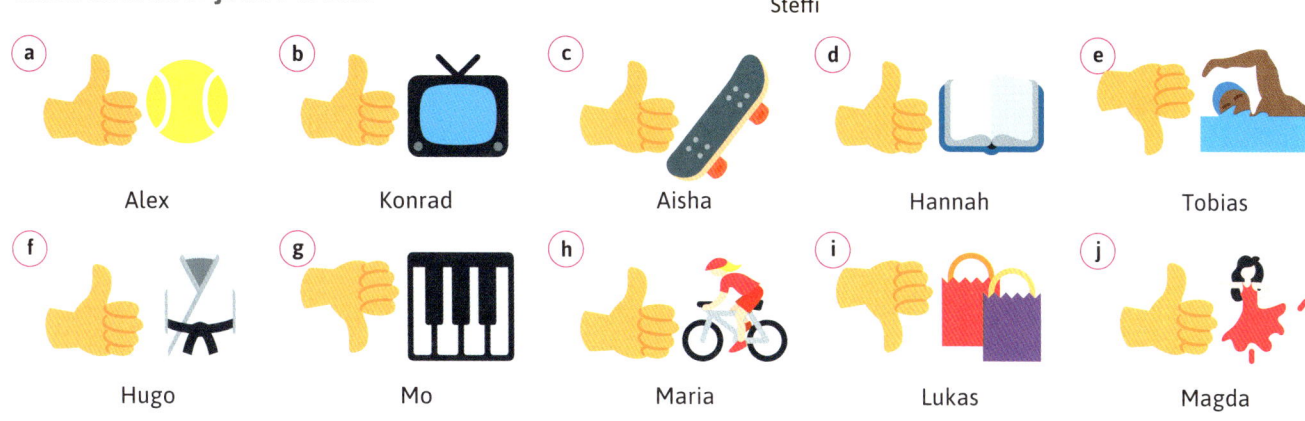

Beispiel: 👍 🥁 *Steffi spielt gern Schlagzeug.*
Steffi

a 👍 🎾 Alex
b 👍 📺 Konrad
c 👍 🛹 Aisha
d 👍 📖 Hannah
e 👎 🏊 Tobias
f 👍 🥋 Hugo
g 👎 🎹 Mo
h 👍 🚴 Maria
i 👎 🛍️ Lukas
j 👍 💃 Magda

✓ 10

7 Übersetz die Sätze ins Deutsche.

a My favourite sport is football.
b Do you like reading?
c I don't like watching TV.
d Wilhelmina likes dancing, but prefers doing yoga. (2 marks)

✓ 5

Max. ✓ 20 Punkte

Deine Resultate

How many points did you get?

Ask your teacher for the answers. Write down your score out of a total of 20 for Reading. Then do the same for Listening and Writing.

Find the right combination of Bronze, Silver and Gold activities for you on pp.70–71!

Up to 6 points   Well done! Do the Bronze activity in the next section.

7–12 points   Great! Do the Silver activity in the next section.

13–20 points   Fantastic! Do the Gold activity in the next section.

neunundsechzig

3 Vorankommen!

Bronze

1 📖 **Read the descriptions and answer Jonas (J) or Amelie (A).**

Jonas liebt Musik. Er macht gern Selfies und ist oft online. Jeden Tag singt er und er tanzt oft.

Amelie ist sehr sportlich und aktiv. Jeden Tag spielt sie Fußball. In ihrer Freizeit geht sie gern ins Kino.

a Who plays football?
b Who dances often?
c Who likes taking selfies?
d Who sings every day?
e Who loves music?
f Who likes going to the cinema?

2 🎧 **Listen to Otto talking about the activities he likes and dislikes. Copy and complete the table.**

Likes	Dislikes
1, …	

1 judo
2 football
3 shopping
4 cinema
5 reading
6 classical music
7 taking selfies
8 video games

3 ✏️ **Do you like doing these activities? Write a sentence for each in German.**

Example: **a** *Ich gehe gar nicht gern ins Kino.*

a going to the cinema
b reading
c listening to music
d skateboarding
e watching TV
f cycling

Silber

4 📖 **Füll die Lücken aus.** Complete the sentences.

spielen   Handy   gern
Großvater   Rad   faulenzt

Hallo. Ich bin die Heidi und ich wohne mit meinem **1** _____, dem Almöhi in den Alpen. Wir haben hier kein Internet und kein **2** _____. Ich gehe gern klettern und male **3** _____. Am liebsten tanze ich und ich fahre gern **4** _____. Meine bester Freund heißt Peter. Er **5** _____ gern. Wir **6** _____ nie Videospiele.

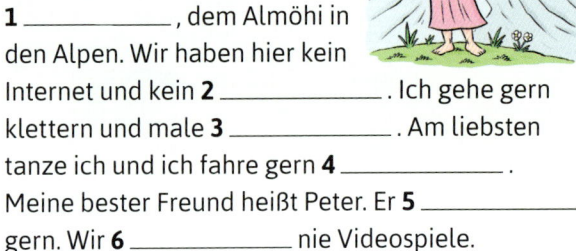

5 🎧 **Listen to Thomas and Tanja talking about their interests. Are the statements true (T) or false (F)?**

a Thomas lives in Austria.
b He plays tennis, badminton and rugby.
c He likes swimming.
d He plays the guitar in a band.
e Tanja finds sport boring.
f She goes online once a week.
g She shares photos and watches videos online.
h Her favourite music is rap.

6 ✏️ **Schreib das Gegenteil!** Write the opposite!

Beispiel: Ich sehe gern fern.
→ Ich sehe nicht gern fern.

a Ich gehe gern einkaufen.
b Ich finde Pop super.
c Ich spiele nicht gern Federball.
d Jeden Tag lese ich.
e Ich habe ein Handy.
f Ich tanze nie.

3 Meine Freizeit

Gold

7 Lies den Blogeintrag und wähl die richtige Antwort.

Sport in der Schweiz

70% der Schweizer und Schweizerinnen treiben Sport. Es gibt zweihundertfünfzig verschiedene Sportarten.

25% aller Schweizer und Schweizerinnen sind in einem Sportclub. Jugendliche machen durchschnittlich 6,6 Stunden pro Woche Sport. Am liebsten spielen sie Fußball oder Eishockey, aber sie schwimmen auch gern und fahren gern Rad.

Wintersportarten sind sehr beliebt, denn es gibt viele Berge und viel Schnee. Zum Beispiel fahren die Schweizer Ski und Snowboard oder sie rodeln.

Bekannte Tennisspieler aus der Schweiz sind Roger Federer und Martina Hingis. Beide haben Grand Slams gewonnen. In 2008 hat die Fußball-Europameisterschaft in der Schweiz und Österreich stattgefunden.

Jugendliche	young people
durchschnittlich	on average
Berge (pl)	mountains
der Schnee	snow
hat ... stattgefunden	took place (perfect tense of *stattfinden*)

a There are **52/250** different types of sports in Switzerland.

b 25 percent of Swiss people **are in a sports club/do exercise**.

c Young people spend on average **66 minutes/6.6 hours** per week doing sport.

d The most popular sports for young people are **football and ice hockey/swimming and cycling**.

e A famous Swiss **tennis player/Olympian** is Martina Hingis.

f In 2008, Switzerland hosted the UEFA European Championship together with **Germany/Austria**.

8 Du hörst eine Radiosendung. Beantworte die Fragen auf Englisch.

a What is the topic of the radio programme?
b What does Rashmi do online? (**two** activities)
c What did she do on Sunday?
d How much time does she spend online?
e What does Peter think about Julien Bam?
f What does he find cool?
g How much time did he spend on the computer on Saturday?

9 Übersetz die Sätze ins Deutsche.

a I like playing the guitar but it is difficult.
b My brother does judo, but I don't like it.
c Every evening I go online and watch video clips.
d I like listening to classical music the most.
e At weekends I go shopping.

10 Schreib einen Text (60–80 Wörter) über deine Freizeitaktivitäten.

- Beschreib was du (nicht) gern machst und warum (..., *denn ich finde es...*).
- Schreib wann du einige Aktivitäten machst.
- Vergleich (*compare*) deine Aktivitäten mit den Aktivitäten eines Freundes/einer Freundin (*Ich mache gern..., aber er/sie macht lieber...*).

🎁 Extra

Use your dictionary skills to look up other activities that interest you which aren't in this book. Remember that the verb will be given in its infinitive form. Irregular verbs are often marked 'irr.' – you can then use a verb table to find the verb form you need.

einundsiebzig

3 Vokabeln

〰️ 3.1 Sport macht Spaß!
Sport is fun!

Welche Sportarten machst du?	Which sports do you do?
der Sport	sport
die Sportart	type of sport

Ich gehe/mache/spiele/tanze…	I go/do/play/dance…
angeln gehen	to go fishing
Ballett tanzen	to dance ballet
Basketball spielen	to play basketball
Federball spielen	to play badminton
ins Fitnesscenter gehen	to go to the gym
Fußball spielen	to play football
Gymnastik machen	to do gymnastics
joggen	to jog
Judo/Karate machen	to do judo/karate
Rugby spielen	to play rugby
schwimmen gehen	to go swimming
Tennis spielen	to play tennis
Yoga machen	to do yoga

Wie findest du…?	How do you find…?
Es ist…	It is…
anstrengend	tiring
entspannend	relaxing
schwierig	difficult
Es macht Spaß.	It is fun.
Es gefällt mir nicht.	I don't like it.

〰️ 3.2 Das mache ich gern!
I enjoy doing that!

Was machst du in deiner Freizeit?	What do you do in your free time?
basteln	to do crafts
einkaufen gehen	to go shopping
faulenzen	to lounge/laze about
fernsehen	to watch television
ins Kino gehen	to go to the cinema
lesen	to read
malen	to paint
mit Freunden chatten	to chat/text with friends
Musik hören	to listen to music
Musik machen	to play/make music
Rad fahren	to ride a bike, to cycle
Skateboard fahren	to go skateboarding
Ski fahren	to ski
Snowboard fahren	to snowboard
tanzen	to dance
Videospiele spielen	to play video games

〰️ 3.3 Hast du Zeit?
Do you have time?

Was machst du oft/nie?	What do you often/never do?
ausruhen/chillen	to relax
die Familienzeit	family time
die Schularbeit	school work
zocken	to game/play video games
zuhause bleiben	to stay at home

ab und zu	now and then
am Wochenende	at the weekend
einmal/zweimal pro Woche	once/twice a week
jeden Abend	every evening
jeden Tag	every day
manchmal	sometimes
nie	never
nur	only
oft	often
selten	rarely
denn	because

72 zweiundsiebzig

3.4 Was für Musik horst du gern?
What kind of music do you like?

die Musik	music
die Musikart	type of music
die elektronische Musik	electronic dance music, electronica
der Hip-Hop	hip-hop
der Indie	indie music
die klassische Musik	classical music
der Pop	pop music
der Rap	rap
der Rock	rock music
der Schlager	German pop
der Techno	techno
der Fan	fan
der/die Komponist/Komponistin	composer
das Lieblingsstück	favourite piece (of music)
das Lied	song
Liedtexte (pl)	song lyrics
die Melodie	melody
der/die Rapper/Rapperin	rapper
der/die Sänger/Sängerin	singer
singen	to sing
der Song	song
die Stimme	voice
aggressiv	aggressive
hart	harsh
inspirierend	inspiring
schön	beautiful
Spielst du ein Instrument?	Do you play an instrument?
Ich bin nicht musikalisch.	I am not musical.
Ich spiele...	I play...
die Geige	violin
die Gitarre	guitar
das Klavier	piano
das Musikinstrument	musical instrument
das Schlagzeug	drums
die Trompete	trumpet

3.5 Stars und Trends – was gibt's Neues?
Stars and trends – what's new?

Abonnenten (pl)	subscribers, followers
eine Million	million/one million
Millionen (pl)	millions
der/die Videoproduzent/Videoproduzentin	video producer/vlogger
Er/Sie macht...	He/She makes...
Kurzfilme (pl)	short films
Sketche (pl)	sketches
Videos (pl)	videos
Er/Sie ist...	He/She is...
beliebt/populär	popular
berühmt	famous
Bilder teilen	to share photos
Fotos liken	to like photos
ein Handy haben	to have a mobile phone
online sein	to be/go online
ein Online-Profil haben	to have a profile online (on a social network)
Selfies machen	to take selfies
Videoclips sehen	to watch video clips
soziale Medien (pl)	social media

4 In der Schule
Los geht's!

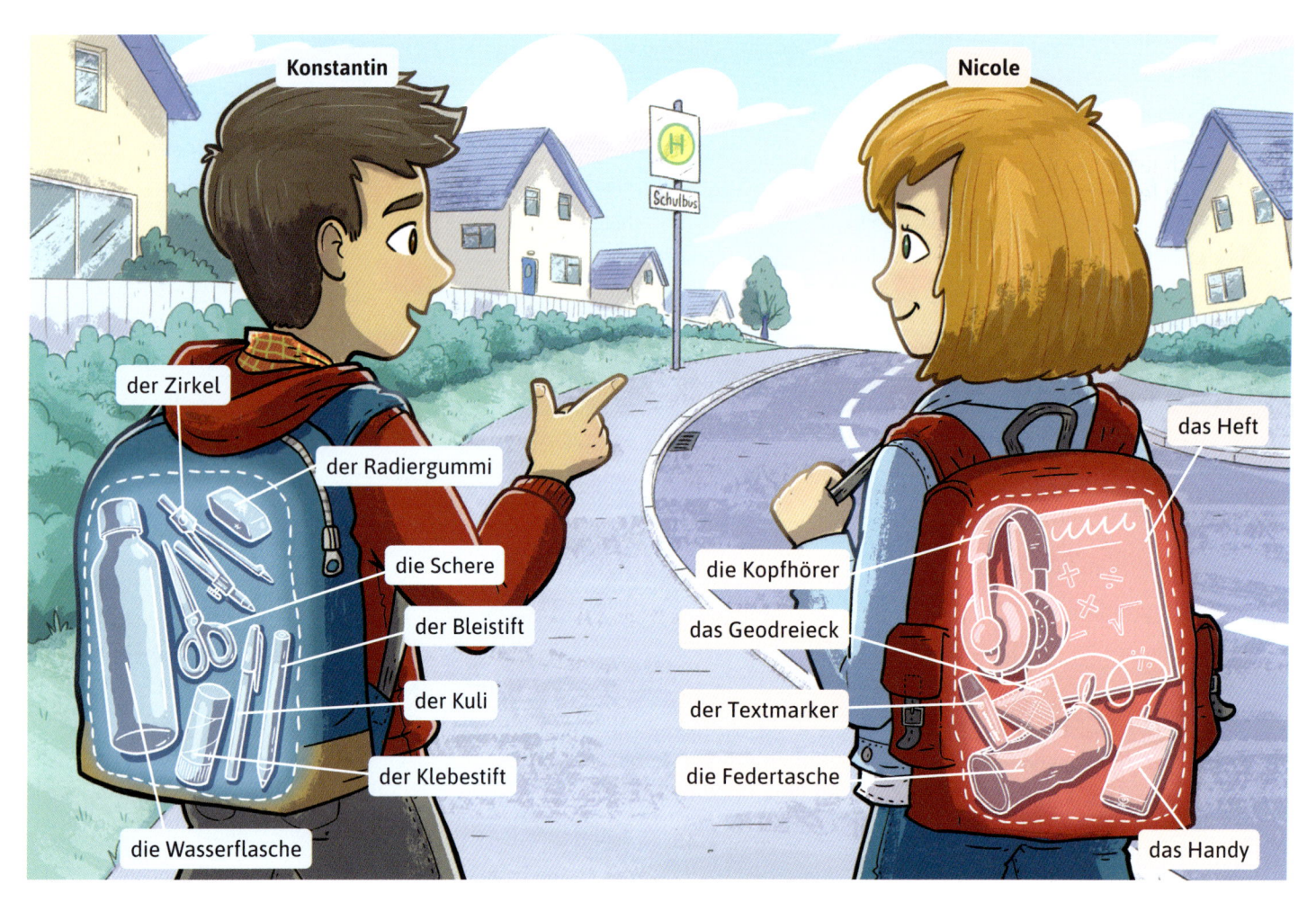

Konstantin
- der Zirkel
- der Radiergummi
- die Schere
- der Bleistift
- der Kuli
- der Klebestift
- die Wasserflasche

Nicole
- das Heft
- die Kopfhörer
- das Geodreieck
- der Textmarker
- die Federtasche
- das Handy

1 👥 Schau die Schultaschen an. Dann deck das Bild zu und nenne so viele Artikel wie möglich. (*Then cover up the picture and name as many items as possible*).

2 👥 Eine Person ist Konstantin und eine Person ist Nicole. Was ist <u>nicht</u> in deiner Tasche? Frag deinen Partner/deine Partnerin danach. Benutz das Tipp-Kästchen zur Hilfe.

Beispiel:
Konstantin: Hast du einen Textmarker?
Nicole: Hier bitte.

Nicole: Ich brauche eine Schere.
Konstantin: Hier bitte.

💡 Tipp
Use these phrases with classmates or your teacher when you need to borrow a piece of equipment. Remember the rule about using *einen* for masculine objects.

Ich brauche einen/eine/ein…
(I need a…)

Hast du einen/eine/ein…?
(Do you have a…? – familiar)

Haben Sie einen/eine/ein…?
(Do you have a…? – formal)

Gib mir bitte deinen/deine/dein…
(Give me your…, please.)

Ich habe meinen/meine/mein … vergessen.
(I have forgotten my…)

Hier bitte.
(Here you are.)

4 In der Schule

3 Translate the school subjects into English.

a Mathematik b Physik c Sport d Englisch
e Musik f Biologie g Religion h Theater

4 Welche Fächer (*school subjects*) magst du? Welche Fächer magst du nicht? Schreib Sätze.

Beispiel:
Ich lerne gern/lieber/am liebsten…
Ich lerne nicht gern…

5 Match the German school terms (1–5) to the English definitions (a–e).

Example: **1** d

1 die Schultüte
2 die Noten
3 der Klassenlehrer/die Klassenlehrerin
4 das Gymnasium
5 der Klassensprecher/die Klassensprecherin

a You don't use this place to exercise! It is a type of school where you can study up to the *Abitur* (German A levels).
b A teacher who is responsible for your form.
c A student who represents your form on the school council.
d A cardboard cone which is filled with stationery and sweets on your first day at primary school.
e The grades you receive after a test and on your school report.

Aussprache

Many school subjects in German are cognates that are similar to the English names for the same subjects. Be careful with pronunciation, though. In German, 'th' is pronounced like a 't'.

Practise saying the words *Mathe* and *Theater*.

Kultur

All children in Germany start school at *eine Grundschule* (a primary school) at six years old.

After *Grundschule* pupils in Germany can go to a *Mittelschule*, *Realschule*, a *Hauptschule*, a *Gesamtschule* or a *Gymnasium*. These are all forms of secondary school.

In Germany, school starts and finishes much earlier than in the UK. Typically, lessons start at 7.45 a.m. and finish at 1 p.m.

fünfundsiebzig

4.1 Heute habe ich Geschichte!

Objectives
- Talking about school subjects
- Telling the time
- Identifying patterns

🎧 Hören

1 Hör zu. Welche Fächer hörst du (1–12)?

Beispiel: **1** i

a Mathematik
b Englisch
c Deutsch
d Französisch
e Spanisch
f Naturwissenschaften (Biologie, Chemie und Physik)
g Geschichte
h Erdkunde
i Sport
j Musik
k Kunst
l Informatik

📖 Lesen

2 Read the texts and answer Mila (M) or Ben (B).

a Who has two foreign languages on one day?
b Who has a favourite day?
c Who mentions German as his/her favourite subject?
d Who finds history and art terrible?

Montag ist mein Lieblingstag. Ich habe sechs Stunden, zum Beispiel Mathe, Erdkunde und Deutsch. Deutsch ist mein Lieblingsfach. **Mila**

Am Mittwoch habe ich fünf Stunden. Ich habe zum Beispiel Französisch und Spanisch und das finde ich total gut, aber dann habe ich auch Geschichte und Kunst und ich finde sie schrecklich. **Ben**

Stunden (pl)	lessons
zum Beispiel	for example
dann	then

🎁 Extra

When you want to talk about modern foreign languages in general, you can use the term *Fremdsprachen*. You may also find *Latein*, *Sozialkunde* and *Werken* on a German timetable. Can you work out what any of these school subjects mean in English? Use a dictionary to check.

⚙ Strategie

Identifying patterns

Some school subjects have the same endings, such as *-kunde* or *-wissenschaft*. These are all feminine words and, in fact, if a noun has either of these endings, it has to be feminine. Try to discover similar patterns as you learn new vocabulary. Can you spot another pattern to do with articles (*der/die/das*) and school subjects?

4 In der Schule

Sprechen

3 👥 **Macht einen Dialog mit euren eigenen Details (*with your own details*).**

Beispiel:
- Was hast du am Montag/Dienstag/Mittwoch…?
- Ich habe am Montag sechs Stunden. Ich habe zum Beispiel…
- Welches Fach lernst du gern?
- Ich lerne gern…, denn es ist interessant.
- Welches Fach lernst du nicht gern?
- Ich lerne nicht gern…, denn es ist langweilig.

Hören

4 🎵 **Listen and read the timetable. Are the lesson times you hear (1–8) true (T) or false (F)?**

Example: **1** T

Mein Stundenplan			
	Uhrzeit	**Montag**	**Dienstag**
1. Stunde	8:00–8:45	Deutsch	c _____
2. Stunde	8:45–9:30	a _____	Informatik
Pause	9:30–9:45		
3. Stunde	9:45–10:30	Sport	d _____
4. Stunde	10:30–11:15	Informatik	e _____
Mittagspause	11:15–11:45		
5. Stunde	11:45–12:30	b _____	Biologie
6. Stunde	12:30–13:15	Englisch	f _____

5 🎵 **Hör zu. Füll die Lücken in dem Stundenplan aus Aktivität 4 mit den richtigen Fächern (a–f) aus.**

Beispiel: **a** Geschichte

Grammatik
WB p.39

Telling the time

The clock image below shows how you tell the time in German. Use *nach* for minutes past the hour. Use *vor* for minutes 'to' the hour (*vor* means 'before'). Add *um* before the time when you are explaining at what time something happens.

- *Es ist neun Uhr.* (It is nine o'clock.)
- *Es ist Viertel nach neun.* (It is quarter past nine.)
- *Es ist Viertel vor zehn.* (It is quarter to ten.)

In German, *halb* expresses the idea of 'half <u>to</u>' the hour (rather than 'half past'), so you need to think ahead to the next full hour.

- *Die zweite Stunde beginnt um **halb zehn**.* (The second lesson begins at **half past nine**.)

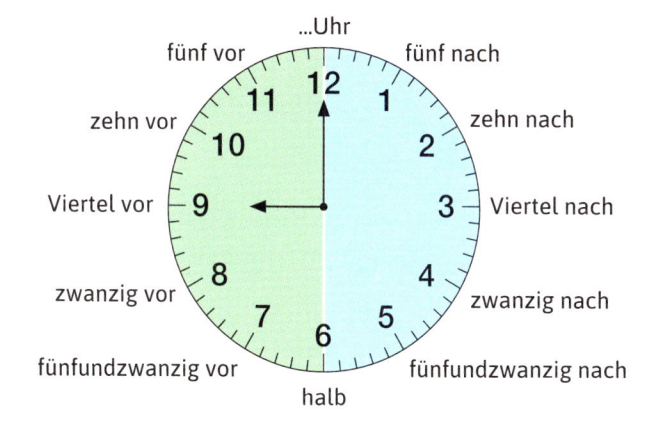

Schreiben

6 Schreib über deine Schule. Beantworte die Fragen auf Deutsch.

Beispiel: **a** Die erste Stunde beginnt um…

- **a** Wann beginnt die erste Stunde?
- **b** Wann endet die zweite Stunde?
- **c** Wann beginnt die Pause?
- **d** Wann beginnt die Mittagspause?
- **e** Wann beginnt die fünfte Stunde?
- **f** Wann endet die Schule?

siebenundsiebzig

4.2 Mathe macht Spaß!

Objectives
- Giving opinions of school subjects
- Using subordinate clauses with *weil*
- Using colloquial expressions

Lesen

1 Lies Maikes Blogeintrag und finde die passenden Sätze (a–f) auf Deutsch.

Hi Leute. Ich bin Maike alias Mathegenie. Ich mag alle meine Fächer. Meine Lieblingsfächer sind Naturwissenschaften. Zum Beispiel interessieren mich Chemie und Physik total. Ich bin stark in Chemie. Ich lerne auch gern Erdkunde. Ich bin schwach in Englisch, aber mir gefallen Fremdsprachen. Nur Sport finde ich schlecht – Sport interessiert mich gar nicht!

a I like all my subjects.
b I am good at Chemistry.
c I also like studying geography.
d I am weak in English…
e …but I like languages.
f Sport doesn't interest me at all!

Sprechen

2 Macht einen Dialog. Benutz positive und negative Ausdrücke (*positive and negative expressions*) aus Maikes Blogeintrag.

Sprachmuster

Das gefällt mir means 'that appeals to me' or 'I like it'. Note that the plural form is *gefallen* and that you can put *mir* at the start of the phrase instead: *Mir gefallen Fremdsprachen. Mir gefällt zum Beispiel Französisch.*

🙂 Mir gefällt Biologie.

🙂 Spanisch interessiert mich.

😞 Ich mag Musik gar nicht.

😞 Und ich finde Naturwissenschaften schlecht.

Übersetzen

3 Translate the adjectives into English and organise them into two groups: positive and negative.

interessant   ätzend   nützlich
langweilig   schwierig   praktisch
prima   einfach   bescheuert
wichtig   anstrengend nervig
unwichtig   spannend

Tipp

Sometimes you might not remember the word you need (for example, *schwierig* for 'difficult') but you might remember an 'antonym' which means the opposite, such as *einfach*. Instead of saying that something is difficult, you could say that it's *nicht einfach*. Which other pairs of antonyms can you find in activity 3?

4 In der Schule

🎧 Hören

4 Listen to eight students describing school subjects. Copy and complete the table in English.

	Subject	Opinion
1	German	interesting

✏️ Schreiben

5 Bring die Wörter in die richtige Reihenfolge.

a Mir gefällt Erdkunde,
  es   weil   interessant   ist.

b Ich bin schwach in Mathe,
  weil   schwierig   ist   es.

c Ich bin stark in Spanisch,
  einfach   ich   weil   es   finde.

d Ich mag Sport nicht,
  anstrengend   zu   es   ist   weil.

e Kunst und Musik interessieren mich,
  weil   voll   sie   kreativ   sind.

🎧 Hören

6 Hör zu und füll die Lücken aus.

Beispiel: **1** Fächer

> Von: farid@echtmail.de
>
> Hallo. Ich gehe in die achte Klasse des Goethe-Gymnasiums. Ich habe sechzehn **1** _____ in der Schule. Ich mag **2** _____ , aber Französisch gefällt mir nicht, weil es **3** _____ ist. Mein Lieblingsfach ist Sport, weil es interessant ist und ich **4** _____ bin. Mein Lehrer ist auch voll **5** _____ . Was ist dein Lieblingsfach? Welche Fächer magst du nicht?

Ich gehe in die siebte/achte/neunte Klasse.
I am in Year 7/8/9.

⚙️ Strategie

Using colloquial expressions

You have already used intensifiers such as *sehr* and *ziemlich*. In everyday, spoken German you will often hear *mega* or *voll*: *Deutsch finde ich mega wichtig, aber Französisch ist voll schwierig*. Practise using everyday language to sound more 'German'!

The word *krass* can have a positive or negative meaning. Can you think of any slang words in English which behave like *krass*?

Aa Grammatik   p.88; WB p.41

Using *weil*

The word *weil* ('because') can be used to combine two separate sentences or 'clauses'. In Unit 3, you saw another word for 'because' (*denn*). The word *weil* is different because it sends the verb to the end of the sentence.

Mein Lieblingsfach ist Spanisch. Es ist interessant. →
*Mein Lieblingsfach ist Spanisch, **weil** es interessant ist.*

Mir gefallen Mathe und Physik. Sie sind wichtig. →
*Mir gefallen Mathe und Physik, **weil** sie wichtig sind.*

Note that there is always a comma before *weil*.

🔄 Übersetzen

7 Translate the email from activity 6 into English.

💬 Sprechen

8 👥 Macht ein Interview.

- In welche Schule und Klasse gehst du?
- Wie viele Fächer hast du?
- Was ist dein Lieblingsfach und warum?
- Welche anderen Fächer magst du und warum?
- Welche Fächer magst du nicht und warum?

✏️ Schreiben

9 Schreib deine Antworten aus Aktivität 8 auf.

4.3 Deutsch lernen – eine gute Idee!

Objectives
- Talking about learning habits and teachers
- Using impersonal expressions
- Revising vocabulary

Lesen

1 Match the statements (1–6) to the people.

Example: **1** Max

1. It is totally fascinating to research information online.
2. It is important to ask questions.
3. It is fun to learn with friends.
4. It is unimportant to learn texts off by heart.
5. It is annoying to do homework.
6. It is a bad idea to cheat.

- Es ist total faszinierend, im Internet zu forschen. — **Max**
- Es ist nervig, Hausaufgaben zu machen. — **Julia**
- Es ist unwichtig, Texte auswendig zu lernen. — **Anja**
- Es ist wichtig, Fragen zu stellen. — **Felix**
- Es ist eine schlechte Idee, zu spicken. — **Mehmet**
- Es macht Spaß, mit Freunden zu lernen. — **Leonie**

Schreiben

2 Bring die Wörter in die richtige Reihenfolge.

a Es ist total unwichtig, Notizen machen zu.
b Es macht Spaß, lernen zu mit Freunden.
c Es ist langweilig, zu Hausaufgaben machen.
d Es ist wichtig, Texte auswendig lernen zu.
e Es ist eine schlechte Idee, Fragen keine stellen zu.
f Es ist eine gute Idee, Vokabeln lernen zu jeden Tag.

Grammatik   p.89; WB p.43

Impersonal expressions

Impersonal expressions present an idea as a generally accepted view rather than a personal opinion: for example, 'It is important to ask questions.' In German, impersonal expressions start with *Es...* and the action (e.g. to ask questions) is described using *zu* and the infinitive form of the verb:

Es ist wichtig, Fragen zu stellen.

4 In der Schule

📖 Lesen

3 Match the English translations (1–8) to the German statements (a–h).

Example: **1** b

1 My teacher is strict.
2 My teacher is helpful.
3 My teacher is very creative.
4 My teacher is very likeable.
5 I think my teacher is quite nice.
6 My French teacher gives a lot of homework.
7 My German teacher is very funny.
8 My teachers give bad grades.

a Mein Lehrer ist sehr sympathisch.
b Meine Lehrerin ist streng.
c Mein Lehrer ist sehr kreativ.
d Meine Französischlehrerin gibt viele Hausaufgaben auf.
e Ich denke, mein Lehrer ist ganz nett.
f Mein Deutschlehrer ist sehr lustig.
g Meine Lehrerin ist hilfsbereit.
h Meine Lehrerinnen geben schlechte Noten.

🔡 Sprachmuster

In German, a female teacher is *die Lehrerin* and a male teacher is *der Lehrer*. The plurals are *Lehrerinnen* and *Lehrer*.

💬 Sprechen

4 „Wie findest du deine Lehrer/Lehrerinnen?" Macht eine Diskussion in kleinen Gruppen.

Mein Deutsch-/Englisch-/Mathelehrer	ist sind	nett. sympathisch. unfreundlich. hilfsbereit.	
Meine Deutsch-/Englisch-/Mathelehrerin	gibt geben	zu viele Hausaufgaben	auf.
Meine Lehrer/Lehrerinnen		schlechte Noten.	

⚙ Strategie

Revising vocabulary

Test yourself on the vocabulary you're learning and try to recycle it later in new contexts. For example, when you describe teachers, you can use other personality adjectives from Unit 2 (*intelligent, dynamisch*), and you could add some detail about what they look like.

🎧 Hören

5 Hör zu. Karim spricht über seine Schule. Wähl die richtige Antwort.

Beispiel: **a** Karim geht auf eine **Gesamtschule**.

a Karim geht auf eine **Gesamtschule/Hauptschule/Realschule**.
b Karims Lieblingsfach ist **Erdkunde/Sozialkunde/Sport**.
c Karim hat in Geschichte **einen netten Lehrer/einen strengen Lehrer/viele Hausaufgaben**.
d Karim findet Schreiben und Lesen **einfach/schwierig/lustig**.
e Er findet es wichtig, **jeden Tag zu lernen/Freunde zu treffen/Notizen zu machen**.
f Karim ist **lustig/entspannt/gestresst**.

eine Lese-Rechtschreib-Schwäche   dyslexia

✏ Schreiben

6 Schreib etwas über deine Lehrer und Lehrerinnen. Beantworte folgende Fragen:

- Hast du einen Lieblingslehrer/eine Lieblingslehrerin? Wie ist er/sie?
- Wie ist dein idealer Lehrer/deine ideale Lehrerin?

einundachtzig **81**

4.4 Was gibt es in deiner Schule?

Objectives
- Talking about what your school is like
- Using *man* with modal verbs
- Understanding cultural differences

📖 Lesen

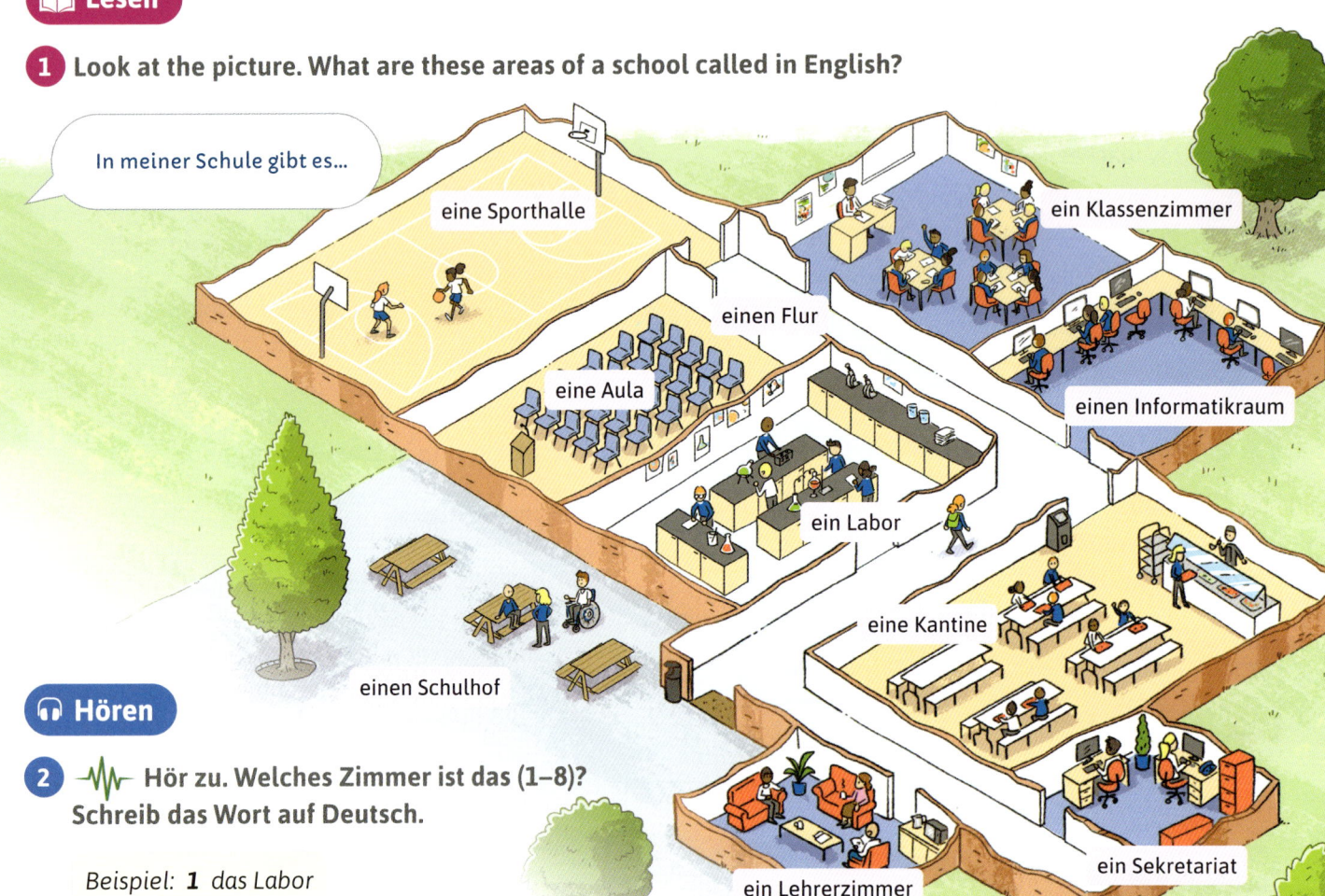

1 Look at the picture. What are these areas of a school called in English?

In meiner Schule gibt es…

- eine Sporthalle
- eine Aula
- einen Flur
- ein Klassenzimmer
- einen Informatikraum
- ein Labor
- eine Kantine
- einen Schulhof
- ein Lehrerzimmer
- ein Sekretariat

🎧 Hören

2 〰️ Hör zu. Welches Zimmer ist das (1–8)? Schreib das Wort auf Deutsch.

Beispiel: **1** das Labor

3 〰️ Hör zu. Ist alles richtig?

💬 Sprechen

4 👥 Was gibt es in eurer Schule? Erstellt eine Liste. Partner A beginnt, dann gibt Partner B noch ein Wort dazu (*adds another word*) und so weiter.

Beispiel:
- In meiner Schule gibt es einen Schulhof.
- In meiner Schule gibt es einen Schulhof und eine Kantine.
- In meiner Schule gibt es einen Schulhof, eine Kantine und…

⚙️ Strategie

Understanding cultural differences

Showing a knowledge of cultural differences will make you stand out. What have you learnt about school life in German-speaking countries so far?

In meiner Schule gibt es	einen/keinen	Flur/Informatikraum/Kunstraum.
	eine/keine	Aula/Kantine/Sporthalle.
	ein/kein	Lehrerzimmer/Sekretariat/Klassenzimmer/Labor/Musikzimmer.

82 zweiundachtzig

4 In der Schule

📖 Lesen

5 Lies die Schulregeln und Schulrechte (*school rules and school rights*). Schreib die Tabelle ab und füll sie aus.

Schuluniform tragen	kein Make-up tragen
in der Kantine essen	mit dem Vertrauenslehrer sprechen
pünktlich sein	Hausaufgaben machen
~~keinen Kaugummi kauen~~	einen Klassensprecher haben
nicht mobben	~~Klassenfahrten machen~~
im Flur nicht rennen	im Unterricht Wasser trinken

Man muss…	Man kann…	Man darf…
	Klassenfahrten machen	keinen Kaugummi kauen

👋 Kultur

Students can take on additional roles and responsibilities in German schools, such as *der Klassensprecher/die Klassensprecherin* (form rep.) or *der Schulsprecher/die Schulsprecherin* (school rep.). A teacher can act as *der Vertrauenslehrer/die Vertrauenslehrerin*, literally 'the teacher you trust'. Students can see their *Vertrauenslehrer/Vertrauenslehrerin* if they have any problems in school or at home.

6 Finde die passenden Verben (a–f) auf Deutsch aus Aktivität 5 und der Grammatik.

Beispiel: **a** trinken

a to drink
b to have
c to use
d to wear
e to do
f to run

Aa Grammatik

p.89; WB p.45

Using *man muss, man kann* and *man darf*

The German word for 'one' or 'you' in the general sense is *man*, and it takes the same verb form as *er, sie* and *es*. We use modal verbs to express what you must do (*Man muss…*), what you can do (*Man kann…*), and what you are allowed to do (*Man darf…*). When you use a modal verb, you have to put a second verb at the end of the sentence in the infinitive form.

*Man **muss** pünktlich **sein**.*
(You **must be** punctual.)

*Man **kann** seine eigene Kleidung **tragen**.*
(You **can wear** your own clothes.)

To talk about what you must not do, use *Man darf…* in the negative.

*Man **darf** das Handy nicht **benutzen**.*
(You **are not allowed to use** a mobile phone.)

💬 Sprechen

7 👥 Was sind die Regeln in eurer Schule? Welche Regeln sind gut und welche Regeln sind schlecht?

Beispiel:

Eine gute Regel ist: Man darf nicht mobben.

Eine schlechte Regel ist: Man muss pünktlich sein.

🙂 Man darf nicht mobben.

😩 Man muss pünktlich sein.

4.5 Welche AG machst du?

Objectives
- Talking about after-school activities
- Revising the 'verb-second' rule
- Developing translation skills

Lesen

1 Was passt zusammen? Verbinde die AGs (1–12) mit den Bildern (a–l).

1 der Chor
2 die Leichtathletik-AG
3 die Umwelt-AG
4 die Anti-Mobbing-AG
5 die Bastel-AG
6 die Schach-AG
7 die Informatik-AG
8 die Theater-AG
9 die Streetdance-AG
10 die Fußball-AG
11 die Film-AG
12 die Hausaufgaben-AG

Beispiel: **1** h

die AG (Arbeitsgemeinschaft) after-school club

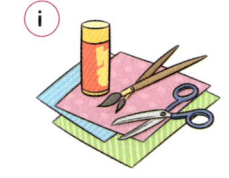

Hören

2 Hör zu. Welche AG aus Aktivität 1 (a–l) sind gut für sie (1–8)?

Beispiel: **1** h

Sprechen

3 „Wer bist du?" Macht Dialoge. Benutz die Informationen in den Kästchen.

Beispiel:
- Ich gehe jeden Montag in die Leichtathletik-AG.
- Du bist Hannes.

Ich gehe	am Montag	in den	Chor.
Ich besuche	jeden Donnerstag einmal pro Woche um vier Uhr nachmittags	in eine/in die	Umwelt-AG, Theater-AG, Film-AG, etc.
Ich habe Wir haben		eine/die	

Hannes
Monday: athletics
Wednesday: film

Kemi
Thursday: choir
Friday: environmental action group

Malik
Tuesday: streetdance
Thursday: anti-bullying club

Heike
Thursday: homework club
Friday: computing club

4 In der Schule

📖 Lesen

4 Lies die E-Mail. Richtig (R) oder falsch (F)?

Beispiel: **a** R

Von:

Hallo. Ich bin Leonard und gehe in die Wittelsbacher-Schule. Mir gefällt meine Schule. Wir haben so viele AGs! Jeden Nachmittag können wir in drei oder vier AGs gehen. Ich bin ziemlich sportlich. <u>Am Dienstag besuche ich eine Basketball-AG, weil das mein Lieblingssport ist und am Donnerstag gehe ich in die Schwimm-AG. Das ist voll anstrengend, macht aber Spaß.</u>

<u>Mein Freund Kai ist ziemlich schwach in Englisch und am Mittwoch gebe ich Kai Nachhilfe in Englisch.</u>

Hast du auch AGs in der Schule? Was machst du nach der Schule?

---

a Leonard mag seine Schule.
b Er hat nicht viele AGs in der Schule.
c Leonard ist unsportlich.
d Leonard macht zweimal pro Woche eine Sport-AG.
e Sein Freund Kai ist total gut in Englisch.
f Leonard gibt Nachhilfe in Mathe.

🎭 Kultur

In Germany, older students often help younger students with their subjects. This is called *Nachhilfe* ('extra coaching/tuition'). Sometimes it's free; sometimes the older students are paid for helping.

🔄 Übersetzen

5 Translate the <u>underlined</u> sentences from activity 4 into English.

⚙ Strategie

Developing translation skills

When you translate into German or English, don't leave out any words and make sure that your grammar is accurate. Sometimes word order can be flexible: 'On Monday I go to a drama club.' means the same as 'I go to a drama club on Monday.' Sometimes you might need to change a German expression in order to make it sound more natural in English. *Es macht Spaß.* translates as 'It ~~makes~~ **is** fun.' *Es ist total anstrengend.* could become 'It's ~~totally~~ **really** hard work.'

✏ Schreiben

6 Schreib die Sätze mit den Zeitadverbien am Anfang *(with the time expression at the beginning)*.

Beispiel: **a** Jeden Tag besuche ich eine AG.

a Ich besuche <u>jeden Tag</u> eine AG.
b Ich gehe <u>am Nachmittag</u> in die Deutsch-Nachhilfe.
c Wir haben <u>nach der Schule</u> viele Sport- und Musik-AGs.
d Laura besucht <u>am Donnerstag</u> eine Umwelt-AG.

Aa Grammatik p.88; WB p.47

The 'verb-second' rule (revision)

Remember that the verb in German has to be the second <u>idea</u> in a sentence, not necessarily the second <u>word</u>.

1st idea	2nd idea	Remaining ideas
Ich	**gehe**	am Nachmittag in eine Theater-AG.
Am Nachmittag	**gehe**	ich in eine Theater-AG.

7 Was machst du? Schreib Sätze mit den Zeitadverbien. Beschreib deine Schulfächer, deine AGs und deine Hobbys.

- am Abend
- zweimal pro Woche
- jeden Mittwoch
- am Wochenende

fünfundachtzig

4 Kultur

Schulleben in deutschsprachigen Ländern

📖 Lesen

1 Lies den Text und finde die passenden Ausdrücke (a–f) auf Deutsch.

Beispiel: **a** *Viele Länder haben eine Schuluniform.*

Uniform? Nein, danke!

Viele Länder haben eine Schuluniform, aber es gibt generell keine Uniform in Deutschland. Die erste deutsche Schule mit einer Schuluniform war im Jahr 2000 eine Schule in Hamburg.

Es gibt wenige Schulen mit Schulkleidung, zum Beispiel einem T-Shirt oder einem Pulli. Schulkleidung ist aber keine Schuluniform, weil die Regeln nicht so streng sind. Schulkleidung hat zum Beispiel nur eine bestimmte Farbe und ein Logo, das T-Shirt ist also rot oder blau und ist mit dem Schullogo bedruckt. Oft kann man die Schulkeidung tragen, aber man muss es nicht.

a Many countries have a school uniform.
b Generally there is no school uniform in Germany.
c because the rules aren't so strict
d a particular colour
e with the school logo
f Often, you can wear the school clothing, but you don't have to.

🎧 Hören

2 Listen to Leonie and answer the questions in English.

a In which country does Leonie live?
b Which year is Leonie in?
c How many national languages does she have in school?
d What does she say about French?
e Which other language does she learn at school, apart from French and German?
f What does she say about this language? (<u>two</u> details)
g Which other language would she like to learn?
h Why does does she want to learn this language?

Switzerland has four national languages: German, French, Italian and Romansh. German, French and Italian are all official languages. Which language you speak in everyday life depends very much on which canton (Swiss region) you live in. Many Swiss people speak at least two of these languages, but also learn English at school.

Did you know that Switzerland has no official capital? Bern is generally said to be the capital city, though.

4 In der Schule

Ski-Akademie Neuschnee Stundenplan	
7:00–7:45 Uhr	Frühstück
8:00–12:30 Uhr	Unterricht
ab 12:40 Uhr	Mittagessen
14:00–18:30 Uhr	Training
ab 18:30 Uhr	Abendessen
19:45–21:15 Uhr	Studium
21:15–22:00 Uhr	Freizeit
ab 22:00 Uhr	Schlafenszeit

Ich gehe in ein Internat für Skisportler in Österreich. Das ist ein typischer Schultag für mich.

ab ... bis (Uhr)   from ... until (o'clock)
das Internat   boarding school

Lesen

3 Lies den Stundenplan und beantworte die Fragen mit den richtigen Zeiten.

Beispiel: **a** *ab 8:00 Uhr bis 12:30 Uhr*

a Wann muss man lernen?
b Wann kann man essen?
c Wann hat man Freizeit?
d Wann muss man schlafen?
e Wann muss man trainieren?

4 Was passt zusammen? Verbinde die Fragen (1–8) mit den Antworten (a–h).

1 In welche Schule gehst du?
2 In welche Klasse gehst du?
3 Wo wohnst du?
4 Wann beginnt der Schultag?
5 Was ist dein Lieblingsfach?
6 Wann trainierst du?
7 Was machst du in deiner Freizeit?
8 Wie findest du deinen Schultag?

a Mein Lieblingsfach ist Sport.
b Ich gehe in eine Ski-Akademie.
c Ich wohne in einem Internat.
d Ich fahre natürlich Ski oder höre Musik.
e Mein Schultag ist anstrengend.
f Ich trainiere am Nachmittag vier Stunden.
g Ich gehe in die achte Klasse.
h Mein Schultag beginnt um 7:30 Uhr.

Übersetzen

5 Translate sentences a–h from activity 4 into English.

Example: **a** *My favourite subject is PE.*

4 Sprachlabor

Word order with time expressions (revision)

As you saw in Unit 3, the verb is always the second idea in a typical sentence. This means that you can choose to put a time expression such as *immer, am Montag, um acht Uhr* or *dann* at the beginning of a sentence or after a verb, as long as the verb always remains the second idea.

1st idea	2nd idea	Remaining ideas
Ich	habe	um acht Uhr Mathematik.
Um acht Uhr	habe	ich Mathematik.
Wir	haben	jeden Tag Hausaufgaben.
Jeden Tag	haben	wir Hausaufgaben.

1 Rewrite the sentences. Start each sentence with the time expression in bold.

Example: **a** *Ich habe um neun Uhr Mathe.*
→ *Um neun Uhr habe ich Mathe.*

a Ich habe **um neun Uhr** Mathe.
b Die Schule beginnt **um halb acht**.
c Wir haben **dann** eine Doppelstunde Deutsch.
d Er hat **am Montag** kein Englisch.
e Die Pause endet **um Viertel nach elf**.
f Sie geht **am Nachmittag** nach Hause.

2 Put the words in the correct order to write two new sentences: one with the time expression <u>at the beginning of the sentence</u> and the other with the time expression <u>after the verb</u>.

a Uhr habe um zehn Pause ich.
b er um ein Sport hat Uhr.
c die Stunde endet nach um Viertel dritte zehn.
d Geschichte sie lernen dann.

Word order after *weil*

Use *weil* ('because') to back up your opinion with a reason. The word *weil* is different from other conjunctions such as *und* and *denn* because it sends the verb to the end of the sentence. This is because *weil* introduces a 'subordinate clause' (a sentence which cannot stand alone). Remember to put a comma before *weil*.

- *Ich finde Mathe gut. Es **ist** interessant.* →
  *Ich finde Mathe gut, weil es interessant **ist**.*
       main clause   subordinate clause

3 Read the pairs of statements. Would they make sense if they were combined into one sentence using *weil*? Write possible (P) or not possible (NP).

a Ich mag Geschichte. Es ist interessant.
b Mein Lieblingsfach ist nicht Deutsch. Ich finde Geschichte schwierig.
c Mein Englischlehrer ist super. Er ist sehr nett.
d Ich mag meine Physiklehrerin Frau Müller. Meine Freundin findet Frau Müller nicht nett.
e Ich finde die Schulregeln unwichtig. Wir haben viele Regeln.
f Die Schulregeln gefallen mir nicht. Sie sind nicht wichtig.

4 Combine the pairs of statements using *weil*. Remember to move the verb in the *weil* clause to the end.

a Ich mag Mathe nicht. Es ist schwierig.
b Mir gefällt Geschichte. Es ist voll super.
c Mein Lieblingsfach ist Erdkunde. Ich finde es wichtig.
d Meine Freundin findet Geschichte gut. Der Lehrer ist nett.
e Sport ist schrecklich. Ich bin nicht sportlich.
f Ich mag Physik nicht. Der Lehrer ist sehr streng.

4 In der Schule

Using *man muss*, *man kann* and *man darf*

The modal verbs *müssen*, *können* and *dürfen* can express what you must do (*Man muss…*), what you can do (*Man kann…*), or what you're allowed to do (*Man darf…*). You also have to use another verb in each sentence to say what it is you must, can or are allowed to do. This verb has to be in the infinitive (*spielen*, *gehen*, *machen*, etc.) and you have to put it at the end of the sentence.

- *Man **muss** Hausaufgaben **machen***. (You **must do** homework.)
- *Man **kann** Spanisch **lernen***. (You **can learn** Spanish.)
- *Man **darf** im Klassenzimmer Wasser **trinken***. (You **are allowed to drink** water in the classroom.)

Be careful with negative forms: to express 'you must not', use *Man darf nicht…*

Man muss nicht… means 'you don't have to (but you can)'.

5 Complete the sentences with the correct form of the modal verb in brackets.

Example: Man kann Projekte machen. (to be able to)

a Man _____ nie das Handy benutzen. (*to be allowed to*)

b Man _____ eine Uniform tragen. (*to have to*)

c Man _____ im Flur nicht rennen. (*to be allowed to*)

d Man _____ auf dem Schulhof essen. (*to be able to*)

e Man _____ in Englisch immer viel schreiben. (*to have to*)

6 Translate the sentences from activity 5 into English.

Impersonal expressions and opinions

Some opinions in German are followed by *zu* + infinitive. You must put a comma in front of the infinitive phrase. These expressions are called impersonal expressions because they present an idea as a general statement, rather than a personal opinion.

- *Es ist interessant, Fremdsprachen zu lernen.* (It is interesting to learn foreign languages.)

7 Translate the sentences into English.

a Es macht Spaß, in die Schule zu gehen.

b Es ist wichtig, Freunde in der Schule zu haben.

c Es ist interessant, Naturwissenschaften zu lernen.

d Es macht Spaß, Klassenfahrten zu machen.

e Es ist nützlich, Informatik zu lernen.

f Es ist gut, einen netten Lehrer zu haben.

Aussprache: u and ü

The German 'u' sound can be long or short like the 'oo' in 'school' or 'book'. The 'ü' with an umlaut can also be long or short. Make a higher 'oo' sound from the front of the mouth, keeping your lips pursed as if you are whistling.

8 Listen and repeat. Then practise with your partner.

fünf   Glück   fünfzehn

Schule   Schülerin   Kunst

Rucksack   Bruder   Mutter

Mütter   dumm   Uhr

9 Practise saying the tongue twister.

Bruder Uwe übt Ukulele, weil Uwes Brüder auch Ukulele üben müssen.

4 Was kann ich schon?

📖 Lesen

1 Was passt zusammen? Verbinde die Fragen (1–10) mit den Antworten (a–j).

1. Wie heißt deine Schule?
2. In welche Klasse gehst du?
3. Was ist in deine Federtasche?
4. Wann beginnt die Schule?
5. Was ist dein Lieblingsfach?
6. Welches Fach magst du nicht?
7. Wie ist dein Mathelehrer?
8. Wie ist deine Deutschlehrerin?
9. Was gibt es in deiner Schule?
10. Was machst du am Nachmittag nach der Schule?

b. Meine Schule heißt Humboldtschule.
c. Mir gefällt Erdkunde nicht.
d. Ich gehe in die siebte Klasse.
e. Es gibt viele Klassenzimmer und eine Aula.
f. Ich habe einen Radiergummi und einen Kuli.
g. Um 8 Uhr.
h. Ich gehe in die Tanz-AG.
i. Mein Lieblingsfach ist Geschichte.
j. Er ist voll streng.

a. Sie ist total hilfsbereit.

✓ 10

2 Read Paul's blog post. Answer the questions in English.

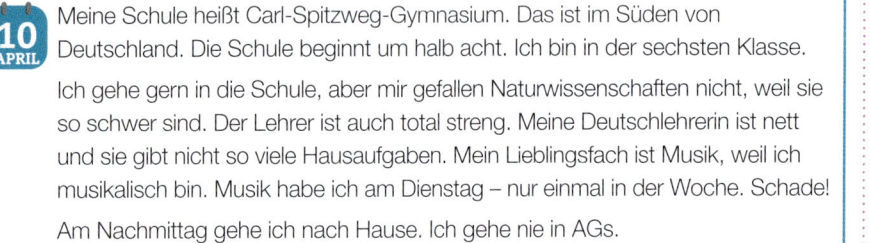

> **10 APRIL**
> Meine Schule heißt Carl-Spitzweg-Gymnasium. Das ist im Süden von Deutschland. Die Schule beginnt um halb acht. Ich bin in der sechsten Klasse.
>
> Ich gehe gern in die Schule, aber mir gefallen Naturwissenschaften nicht, weil sie so schwer sind. Der Lehrer ist auch total streng. Meine Deutschlehrerin ist nett und sie gibt nicht so viele Hausaufgaben. Mein Lieblingsfach ist Musik, weil ich musikalisch bin. Musik habe ich am Dienstag – nur einmal in der Woche. Schade!
>
> Am Nachmittag gehe ich nach Hause. Ich gehe nie in AGs.

a. Where in Germany is Paul's school?
b. When does his school day start?
c. How does he feel about going to school?
d. What does Paul say about science? (2 marks)
e. What does he say about his German teacher? (2 marks)
f. What is Paul's favourite subject?
g. On which day does he have a lesson in his favourite subject?
h. How often does he go to after-school clubs?

✓ 10

Max. ✓ 20 Punkte

🎧 Hören

3 〰️ Listen to teenagers (1–10) talking about school life. Choose the topic (a–f) that each speaker talks about. (You can use each topic more than once.)

a. school subjects
b. school rules
c. school equipment
d. school timetable
e. extra-curricular activities
f. school rooms

✓ 10

4 〰️ Hör zu und beantworte die Fragen auf Deutsch.

a. In welcher Klasse ist Karin?
b. Wie viele Schüler sind in Karins Klasse?
c. Wie ist Karins Klassenzimmer?
d. Wie viele Labors sind in Karins Schule?
e. Was ist Karins Lieblingsfach?
f. Warum mag Karin das Fach?
g. Welches Fach mag sie nicht?
h. Welche Regel nervt Karin am meisten?
i. Wie findet sie AGs?
j. Was hat sie am Dienstag Nachmittag?

✓ 10

Max. ✓ 20 Punkte

4 In der Schule

✎ Schreiben

5 Was hast du in der Schule und wann? Schreib Sätze auf Deutsch.

Beispiel:

08:00 🇪🇸

Ich habe um acht Uhr Spanisch.

a 08:30 🇬🇧
b 09:15 🧮
c 10:45 🇩🇪
d 11:30 🌍
e 12:00 🏐

✓ 10

6 Übersetz den Text ins Deutsche.

I am in Year 7. I have nine subjects, for example German, maths and geography. My favourite subject is English because it is useful. I don't like PE because I am not sporty. My PE teacher is very strict.

✓ 10

Max. ✓ 20 Punkte

Deine Resultate

How many points did you get?

Ask your teacher for the answers. Write down your score out of a total of 20 for Reading. Then do the same for Listening and Writing.

Find the right combination of Bronze, Silver and Gold activities for you on pp.92–93!

Up to 6 points — Well done! Do the Bronze activity in the next section.

7–12 points — Great! Do the Silver activity in the next section.

13–20 points — Fantastic! Do the Gold activity in the next section.

einundneunzig

4 Vorankommen!

Bronze

1 📖 **Read about Lina's school life and answer the questions in English.**

> Ich gehe in die siebte Klasse des Max-Born-Gymnasiums. Die Schule beginnt um Viertel nach acht. Ich habe sechs Stunden am Tag.
> Mein Lieblingsfach ist Kunst, weil ich kreativ bin. Ich mag Erdkunde nicht, weil es langweilig ist. Meine Lehrer sind sehr freundlich, aber ich habe zwei Stunden Hausaufgaben am Tag! Der Schultag endet um halb zwei.

- a Which year is Lina in?
- b How many lessons does she have per day?
- c Why does she not like geography?
- d How much homework does she get per day?
- e When does school end?

2 🎧 **Listen to the opinions about school. Choose the correct answer.**

1. geography – **interesting/difficult**
2. history – **useful/easy**
3. school uniform – **trendy/awful**
4. rules – **fair/too strict**

3 ✏️ **Complete the sentences in German with your own details.**

- a Meine Schule heißt _____ .
  (Give the name of your school.)
- b Mein Lieblingsfach ist _____ , weil es _____ ist.
  (Name your favourite subject and say why.)
- c Der Lehrer/Die Lehrerin ist _____ .
  (Say what the teacher is like.)
- d Ich mag _____ nicht, weil es _____ ist.
  (Name a subject you don't like and say why.)
- e Die Schule beginnt um _____ und endet um _____ .
  (Say what time school starts and finishes.)

Silber

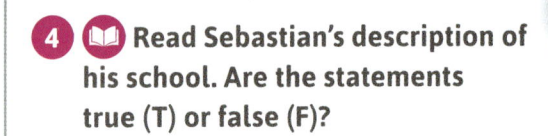

4 📖 **Read Sebastian's description of his school. Are the statements true (T) or false (F)?**

> Ich bin Sebastian und gehe auf ein Gymnasium. Die Schule beginnt um halb acht. Das ist sehr früh, aber das ist kein Problem.
> In der Schule gibt es 22 Klassenzimmer, zwei Labors, einen Informatikraum, ein Lehrerzimmer und ein Sekretariat. Leider gibt es kein Schwimmbad, aber wir haben eine Sporthalle. Wir haben auch eine große Aula.

- a Sebastian's school starts at 8.30 a.m.
- b He does not like the start time.
- c They have a computer room.
- d They have a swimming pool.
- e They have a sports hall.
- f The assembly hall is big.

5 🎧 **Listen to Ahmed explaining his school's rules about various activities. Put the activities in the order you hear them.**

- a using computers
- b being nice to each other
- c using mobile phones
- d wearing own clothes

6 ✏️ **Schreib einen Text (40–60 Wörter) über deine Schule. Schreib etwas über folgende Punkte.** Write a text (40–60 words) about your school. Write about the following points.

- die Schuleinrichtung (*school facilities*)
- deine Schulfächer
- deine Lehrer/Lehrerinnen
- die AGs

4 In der Schule

Gold

7 **Lies Maiks E-Mail über seine Schule und beantworte die Fragen auf Englisch.**

Von: maik@tschues.com

Hallo Jon,

hier ist meine Schule! Es gibt eintausend Schüler und Schülerinnen an meiner Schule. In meiner Klasse – der 8c – sind wir achtundzwanzig. Ich habe viele Freunde in meiner Klasse. Es gibt aber zwei oder drei Schüler, die nicht so nett sind. Alle anderen sind aber sehr hilfsbereit.

Mein Klassenzimmer ist im dritten Stock. Das finde ich anstrengend, weil ich nicht so sportlich bin und man darf den Lift nicht benutzen. Ich habe zehn Fächer in der Schule. Meine Schule ist ganz speziell, denn wir lernen Erdkunde und Geschichte auf Englisch! Das ist manchmal voll schwer aber lustig. Ich lerne viel.

Wie viele Fremdsprachen lernst du?

Gruß,
Maik

im dritten Stock   on the third floor

a How many students are in Maik's school?
b How many students are in his form?
c What does he say about two or three of his classmates?
d What are the others like?
e What does he say about going to his classroom? (**three** details)
f What is special about learning geography and history in his school?
g Which question does Maik ask Jon?

8 **Hör zu und füll die Lücken aus. Du brauchst nicht alle Wörter benutzen.**

wichtig   mitbringen   doof

wählen   nützlich   spielen

essen   trinken   rennen

a Lola findet ihre Schulregeln _____ .
b Sie muss immer alle Hefte und Bücher _____ .
c Die Informatikstunden findet sie _____ .
d Im Informatikraum darf man nicht _____ .
e Im Flur darf man nicht _____ .
f Man kann einen Klassensprecher _____ .

9 **Schreib einen Blogeintrag (zirka 80 Wörter) über dein Schulleben.**

Schreib zum Beispiel etwas über:
- deine Fächer
- deine Lehrer
- die Schulräume
- die Schulregeln.

🎁 Extra

When you write about your school life, try to:
- use at least one time expression at the beginning of a sentence
- give a positive and a negative opinion
- use *denn* and *weil* at least once to give a reason for your opinion
- combine sentences using *und*, *aber* and *oder*.

dreiundneunzig

4 Vokabeln

🎵 4.1 Heute habe ich Geschichte!
I've got history today!

das Fach/Schulfach	subject/school subject
Fächer (pl)	subjects
lernen	to learn, to study
die (Mittags)pause	(lunch) break
die Stunde	lesson
der Stundenplan	timetable

Was hast du am Montag?	What do you have on Monday?
Biologie	biology
Chemie	chemistry
Deutsch	German
Englisch	English
Erdkunde	geography
Französisch	French
Fremdsprachen (pl)	foreign languages
Geschichte	history
Informatik	computing
Kunst	art
Mathematik	maths
Musik	music
Naturwissenschaften (pl)	sciences
Physik	physics
Spanisch	Spanish
Sport	PE

um … (Uhr)	at … (o'clock)
halb neun/zehn/elf…	half past eight/nine/ten…
Viertel vor/nach	quarter to/past (the hour)

dann	then, next
zum Beispiel	for example

🎵 4.2 Mathe macht spaß!
Maths is fun!

Ich bin stark/schwach in…	I am good/bad at…
Deutsch interessiert mich.	German interests me.
Fremdsprachen interessieren mich.	Languages interest me.
Mir gefällt Mathe.	I like maths.
Mir gefallen Kunst und Sport.	I like art and PE.

mega	mega, super
total	totally
voll	really

anstrengend	tiring
ätzend	awful
bescheuert	stupid
einfach	easy
interessant	interesting
langweilig	boring
nervig	annoying
nützlich	useful
praktisch	practical
prima	great
schrecklich	awful
schwierig	difficult
spannend	exciting
(un)wichtig	(un)important

weil	because

Ich gehe in die siebte/achte/neunte Klasse.	I am in Year 7/8/9.

🎵 4.3 Deutsch lernen – eine gute Idee!
Learning German – a good idea!

(Texte) auswendig lernen	to learn (texts) off by heart
eine gute/schlechte Idee	a good/bad idea
faszinierend	fascinating

4 In der Schule

Fragen stellen	to ask questions
Hausaufgaben machen	to do homework
im Internet forschen	to do research online
mit Freunden lernen	to study with friends
Notizen machen	to make notes
spicken	to cheat
Vokabeln lernen	to learn vocabulary
der/die Lehrer/Lehrerin	teacher
Mein Lehrer/Meine Lehrerin gibt zu viele Hausaufgaben auf.	My teacher gives too much homework.
Mein Lehrer/Meine Lehrerin gibt gute/schlechte Noten.	My teacher gives good/bad marks.
hilfsbereit	helpful
nett	nice, friendly
streng	strict
sympatisch	kind
unfreundlich	unfriendly

4.4 Was gibt es in deiner Schule?
What is there in your school?

In meiner Schule gibt es…	In my school there is/are…
die Aula	(assembly) hall
der Flur	corridor
der Informatikraum	computer room
die Kantine	canteen
das Klassenzimmer	classroom
das Labor	science lab
das Lehrerzimmer	staff room
der Schulhof	playground, school yard
das Sekretariat	admin office, secretary's office
die Sporthalle	sports hall
eine gute/schlechte Regel	a good/bad rule
Schulrechte (pl)	school rights
Schulregeln (pl)	school rules
das Handy benutzen	to use your mobile phone
einen Klassensprecher haben	to have a student representative
im Flur rennen	to run in the corridor
im Unterricht Wasser trinken	to drink water in class
Kaugummi kauen	to chew gum
Klassenfahrten machen	to go on school trips
mit dem Vertrauenslehrer sprechen	to speak with the student welfare teacher
mobben	to bully
pünktlich sein	to be punctual/on time
Schuluniform/Make-up tragen	to wear school uniform/make-up
seine eigene Kleidung tragen	to wear your own clothes

4.5 Welche AG machst du?
Which after-school club do you go to?

Was machst du nach der Schule?	What do you do after school?
die AG (= Arbeitsgemeinschaft)	after-school club
Ich besuche die … -AG./ Ich gehe in die … -AG.	I go to … club.
Ich gehe in den Chor.	I go to choir.
die Anti-Mobbing-AG	anti-bullying club
die Bastel-AG	crafts club
der Chor	choir
die Film-AG	film club
die Fußball-AG	football club
die Hausaufgaben-AG	homework club
die Informatik-AG	computing club
die Leichtathletik-AG	athletics club
die Nachhilfe	extra tuition
die Schach-AG	chess club
die Streetdance-AG	streetdance club
die Theater-AG	drama/theatre club
die Umwelt-AG	environmental action group
abends/am Abend	in the evening
nachmittags/am Nachmittag	in the afternoon

5 Mahlzeit!
Los geht's!

1 In welchem Monat hat welches Obst oder Gemüse Saison? *(Which fruit or vegetable is in season in which month?)*

Beispiel: Januar – Orangen

Avocados   Bohnen   Erdbeeren   Granatäpfel   Himbeeren   Kartoffeln
Kohl   Kürbisse   Orangen   Pflaumen   Spargel   Tomaten

Januar	Februar	März	April
Mai	Juni	Juli	August
September	Oktober	November	Dezember

2 Welches Gesicht ist das: a oder b?

1. Er/Sie hat Tomatenaugen.
2. Er/Sie hat Gurkenaugen.
3. Er/Sie hat einen Zucchinimund.
4. Er/Sie hat eine Karottennase.
5. Er/Sie hat Karottenohren.
6. Er/Sie hat einen Tomatenmund.
7. Er/Sie hat eine Auberginennase.

5 Mahlzeit!

3 Read about the treats from German-speaking countries. Copy and complete the table in English.

Treat	Inventor	Place	Year
Gummibärchen			
Mozartkugeln	Paul Fürst		
Ritter Sport		Bad Cannstatt	
Toblerone			1908

Gummibärchen

Im Jahre 1922 erfindet Hans Riegel Gummibärchen in Bonn. **Ha**ns **Ri**egel **Bo**nn – Haribo!

Gummibärchen sind Fruchtgummis. Kleine Teddybärchen, gelb, rot, grün, weiß.

Sie sind fast hundert Jahre alt!

Mozartkugeln

Mozartkugeln sind Süßwaren aus Schokolade, Pistazien, Marzipan und Nougat. Paul Fürst erfindet Mozartkugeln im Jahre 1890 in Salzburg.

Ritter Sport

Alfred und Clara Ritter erfinden Ritter Sport im Jahre 1912 in Bad Cannstatt in Deutschland. Heute gibt es mehr als 30 Sorten!

Toblerone

Theodor Tobler und Emil Baumann erfinden die Toblerone im Jahre 1908 in Bern, in der Schweiz.

Die Toblerone wird vom Matterhorn inspiriert. Sie ist dreieckig!

---

erfinden — to invent, to found
Süßwaren (pl) — confectionery
dreieckig — triangular

Extra
What other facts can you note about the treats from activity 3?

Kultur
Guten Appetit! and *Mahlzeit!* are two phrases which both mean 'Enjoy your meal!' in German. The word *Mahlzeit* means 'meal' or 'mealtime'.

siebenundneunzig 97

5.1 Frühstück – die wichtigste Mahlzeit!

Objectives
- Talking about what you eat and drink
- Using the verbs *essen* and *trinken*
- Reusing language in new contexts

📖 Lesen

1 Was passt zusammen?

1	Brot (n)	7	Marmelade (f)
2	Butter (f)	8	Milch (f)
3	Frühstücksflocken (pl)	9	Müsli (n)
4	Joghurt (m)	10	Obst (n)
5	Käse (f)	11	Schinken (m)
6	Kekse (pl)	12	Wurst (f)
13	Kaffee (m)	15	Tee (m)
14	Saft (m)	16	Wasser (n)

> ⚠️ **Achtung!**
> In German, *die Marmelade* is jam, <u>not</u> marmalade!

🎧 Hören

2 〰️ Hör zu. Was essen und trinken sie zum Frühstück (1–4)? Schreib die richtigen Buchstaben aus Aktivität 1 (a–p) auf.

Beispiel: **1** g, c, …

💬 Sprechen

3 👥 Macht Dialoge.

Beispiel:
- Was isst du zum Frühstück?
- Ich esse … mit … oder…
- Und was trinkst du?
- Ich trinke…
- Was isst du zum zweiten Frühstück?
- Zum zweiten Frühstück esse ich … oder… Ich trinke…

Aa Grammatik p.110; WB p.53

The present tense of *essen* and *trinken*

To form the present tense of *trinken* (to drink), follow the pattern of taking the stem (*trink-*) and adding the usual endings.

ich ___e	wir ___en
du ___st	ihr ___t
er/sie/es ___t	sie/Sie ___en

The verb *essen* (to eat) behaves in a similar way to other irregular verbs you have met such as *fahren* and *lesen*. It has a vowel change in the *du* and *er/sie* forms:

ich esse   du **i**sst   er/sie/es **i**sst

🌐 Kultur

As the school day in Germany starts early, many students take a mid-morning snack (*ein zweites Frühstück* – 'a second breakfast') with them.

5 Mahlzeit!

📖 Lesen

4 Read the interview. Copy and complete the table in English.

Breakfast	Lunch	Dinner	Never eats or drinks
muesli, ...			coffee, ...

gesund	healthy
die Ernährung	diet, eating habits
Nüsse (pl)	nuts
das Hähnchen	chicken
das Gemüse	vegetables
Kartoffeln (pl)	potatoes

Gesund mit Georg! Ein Interview

Hallo Georg. Du bist so gesund! Kannst du uns etwas über deine Ernährung sagen? Was isst und trinkst du zum Frühstück?
Ja, ich bin so gesund! Zum Frühstück esse ich Müsli. Ich trinke Milch. Ich trinke keinen Kaffee. Das ist gar nicht so gesund.

Und zum Mittagessen? Was isst du zum Mittagessen?
Ich esse Brot, Käse und Obst zum Mittagessen. Ich esse auch Nüsse.

Was isst du zum Abendessen?
Zum Abendessen esse ich Fisch oder Hähnchen mit Gemüse und Kartoffeln. Ich trinke auch Wasser. Einen Liter Wasser.
Ich esse keine Hamburger und ich trinke gar keine Cola. Nein, danke! Ich esse kein Junkfood, kein Fastfood. Das ist alles so ungesund.

⚙ Strategie

Reusing language in new contexts

Do you remember the word *kein*, for saying what you don't have?

*Ich habe **keine** Geschwister/Haustiere.*
(I don't have any siblings/pets.)

You also can use *kein* to say what you don't eat or drink:

*Ich esse **kein** Fastfood.*
*Ich trinke **keinen** Kaffee.*

When using language in new contexts, remember that the same grammatical rules apply. Here, you still need to add *-en* to *kein* for masculine singular nouns when they are the object of the sentence.

✏ Schreiben

5 Du bist Ulli und du lebst sehr ungesund. Beschreib deine Ernährung.

Beispiel:
Zum Frühstück esse ich nichts. Ich trinke Kaffee mit Zucker.
Zum Mittagessen esse ich... Ich esse kein...
Zum Abendessen...

🧩 Sprachmuster

The German words for meals are all examples of compound nouns (nouns formed from other words put together).

Breakfast: *Frühstück = früh* ('early') + *Stück* ('piece (of bread)')

Lunch: *Mittagessen = Mittag* ('midday') + *Essen* ('food/to eat')

Which two words form the last meal of the day, *Abendessen*?

💬 Sprechen

6 👥 Macht ein Interview mit Ulli. Benutzt die Fragen in dem Interview aus Aktivität 4 und eure Antworten aus Aktivität 5.

🔄 Übersetzen

7 Translate the article into English.

Ein gutes Frühstück gibt Energie für den Tag!
Hier ist ein typisches Wiener Frühstück:
- Kaffee oder Tee
- Semmel oder Croissant
- Butter
- Honig oder Marmelade

die Semmel	bread roll

5.2 Wie schmeckt's?

Objectives
- Buying food
- Using *mir* and *dir*
- Justifying opinions

Hören

1 Hör zu. Was nehmen sie (1–9)? Was kostet das?

Beispiel: **1** g – 0,89 €

0,69 €   0,79 €

0,89 €   0,99 €

1,05 €   1,09 €

1,29 €   2,59 €

2,99 €

Verkaufsautomaten – hier kann man alles kaufen!

a ein Liter Milch
b 100 Gramm Quark
c eine Scheibe Schinken
d eine Flasche Wasser
e eine Tafel Schokolade
f eine Packung Butterkekse
g eine Dose Cola
h eine Tüte Gummibärchen
i ein Stück Käse

Sprechen

2 Macht sechs Dialoge.

Beispiel:
- Was nimmst du?
- Ich nehme eine Dose Cola.
- Was kostet das?
- Es kostet neunundachtzig Cent.

> **Tipp**
> As with *essen*, the stem of the verb *nehmen* (to take) changes in the *du* and *er/sie/es* forms of the present tense:
> *ich nehme   du nimmst   er/sie/es nimmt*

hundert

5 Mahlzeit!

📖 Lesen

3 Read about the food and drink that Samuel and Ida like and dislike. Copy and complete the table in English.

	Food		Drink	
	✔	✘	✔	✘
Samuel	meat, ...			
Ida				

Ich esse gern Fleisch, weil es mir schmeckt. Ich esse auch gern Reis, aber ich esse nicht gern Salat. So langweilig! Ich trinke gern Cola, denn es schmeckt mir. Ich trinke auch gern Limonade, aber ich trinke nicht gern Tee. Das schmeckt mir gar nicht!

Samuel

Ich esse gern Gemüse mit Nudeln, weil es mir schmeckt. Ich esse auch gern Obst. Eier mag ich nicht. Ich trinke gern Kaffee und auch Wasser, aber ich trinke nicht gern Soda, weil es mir nicht schmeckt.

Ida

Aa Grammatik

WB p.55

Using *mir* and *dir*

In activity 3, you saw the phrases *es schmeckt mir* and *es schmeckt mir nicht*. Roughly translated, these mean 'it tastes good/doesn't taste good to me'.

Schmeckt es dir? Ja, mir schmeckt's.

The words *dir* and *mir* are the dative forms of *du* and *ich*. You will encounter them in other phrases.

Mir ist warm/kalt.	I'm hot/cold. (literally 'It's hot/cold to me.')
Mir geht's gut.	I'm fine/well. (literally 'It goes well to me.')
Gefällt es dir?	Do you like it? (literally 'Is it pleasing to you?')

Note that a phrase can start with *mir* and *dir*, and you can shorten *es* to *'s* after the verb.

⚙ Strategie

Justifying opinions

You've already encountered (*nicht*) *gern*, *lieber* and *am liebsten* for talking about things you like and dislike doing. Use these phrases to talk about eating and drinking, too, backing up your opinions using *denn* and *weil*:

Ich esse gern Käse, denn mir schmeckt's.
Am liebsten trinke ich Wasser, weil es gesund ist.

To say what your favourite food or drink is, use *Mein Lieblingsessen/Mein Lieblingsgetränk ist...*

Mein Lieblingsessen ist Schokolade, denn mir schmeckt's gut!

✏ Schreiben

4 Was isst du gern? Was trinkst du gern? Schreib Sätze.

Was isst/trinkst du gern?	Ich esse/trinke gern...
Was ist dein Lieblingsessen/ Lieblingsgetränk?	Mein Lieblingsessen/ Lieblingsgetränk ist...
Schmeckt dir...?	Ja, mir schmeckt's (gut)./ Nein, mir schmeckt's nicht.

💬 Sprechen

5 👥 Macht Dialoge. Benutzt eure Sätze aus Aktivität 4.

Eier (pl)   Fleisch (n)   Obst (n)   Gemüse (n)

Nudeln (pl)   Reis (m)   Salat (m)   Soda (n)

hunderteins

5.3 Foodtruck-Fieber!

Objectives
- Ordering something to eat
- Using *ich möchte* and *ich hätte gern*
- Dealing with unfamiliar language when listening

📖 Lesen

1 Look at the picture of the street food festival. What can you buy at each food truck? Make notes in English.

Example: **a** vegan hamburgers, ...

a Viktor Vegan – Burger, Currywurst, alles vegan.

b Die feinsten Knödel – pikant oder süß!

c Die Gourmet-Bratwurst – Bratwürste mit Pommes serviert.

d Olaf der Fischer – Fischfilet, Fischbrötchen, Fischburger.

e Der grüne Wagen – Salate und Suppen.

f Bella Pizza – frische Flammkuchen und Pizza!

Knödel (pl)	dumplings
pikant	spicy
süß	sweet
die Bratwurst	fried or grilled sausage
Pommes (pl)	chips
das Brötchen	bread roll

🎧 Hören

2 〰 Hör zu. Bei welchem Foodtruck sind sie (1–6)? Schreib die richtigen Buchstaben aus Aktivität 1 (a–f) auf.

Beispiel: **1** d

🎭 Kultur

Knödel are Austrian dumplings. They can be sweet with fruit (*Marillenknödel/Zwetschgenknödel*) or savoury (*Kartoffelknödel/Fleischknödel*).

Flammkuchen are thin pizzas, often served with soured cream and onions.

5 Mahlzeit!

💬 Sprechen

3 👥 Ihr seid beim Street Food Festival. Macht Dialoge.

Beispiel:
- *Was darf es sein?*
- *Ich möchte.../Ich hätte gern...*

einen	Knödel/Flammkuchen/Salat.
eine	Bratwurst/Currywurst/Suppe/Pizza.
ein	Fischbrötchen.
etwas	Veganes.

🎧 Hören

4 Listen to the orders at the food trucks. Which <u>two</u> food items are <u>not</u> mentioned?

- a sausage
- b dumplings
- c salad
- d soup
- e fries
- f bread
- g pizza

⚙️ Strategie

Dealing with unfamiliar language when listening

Don't panic if you don't understand every word when listening to spoken German.

- Make sure you understand the overall gist of the conversation. Can you work out the missing words by context?
- For any words you don't know, make a note of what the word sounds like. Could it share a root with other German words you do know?
- You might not know exactly what a word means, but you might be able to tell what sort of word it is (for example, noun, adjective, positive, negative). This will help you in developing a response.

🔄 Übersetzen

5 Translate the sentences into English.

- a Was möchtest du essen?
- b Etwas zu trinken?
- c Schmeckt's dir?
- d Ich hätte gern Salat oder Suppe.
- e Lecker! Super lecker!
- f Sonst noch was?

Aa Grammatik   p.110; WB p.57

Using *ich möchte* and *ich hätte gern*

Both *ich möchte* and *ich hätte gern* are useful ways of saying what you would like to have. These use a particular form of the verbs *mögen* (to like) and *haben* (to have).

💬 Sprechen

6 👥 In Gruppen von vier Personen (A–D). Welchen Foodtruck wählt ihr aus?

- **A** = Du isst nicht gern Fisch.
- **B** = Du bist Vegetarier/Vegetarierin.
- **C** = Du lebst sehr ungesund und isst nur Fastfood.
- **D** = Du isst alles.

Beispiel:
A: Hast du Hunger? Was möchtest du?
B: Ich hätte gern einen Salat. Und du?
C: Salat schmeckt mir nicht. Ich möchte...

✏️ Schreiben

7 Beschreib deinen idealen Foodtruck.

Foodtruck-Name:

Zum Essen:

Zum Trinken:

hundertdrei

5.4 Guten Appetit!

Objectives
- Reading restaurant reviews
- Starting to use the perfect tense with *haben*
- Using German creatively

Lesen

1 Lies die Speisekarten (*menus*) und finde die passenden Ausdrücke (a–h) auf Deutsch.

1 Die DEUTSCHE ECKE

Vorspeisen
Salatteller
Melone

Hauptgerichte
Schnitzel mit Pommes
Omelett mit Pilzen und Käse

Nachspeisen
Eis mit Sahne
Zitronentorte

2 Pizzeria Sicilia

Pizza Margherita
Tomatensauce und Käse

Pizza Tonno
Tomatensauce, Käse, Thunfisch und Zwiebeln

Pizza Etna
Tomatensauce, Käse, Paprika und Peperoni

Extra Zutaten
Oliven
Artischocken
Kapern

3 Kartoffelkeller

Vorspeise
Berliner Kartoffelsuppe

Hauptgerichte
Bratwurst mit Sauerkraut und Bratkartoffeln

Kartoffelpfanne „Mumbai" mit Hähnchenbrust, Champignons und Curry

Nachspeisen
Drei Kartoffelpuffer mit Zucker und Zimt

Kartoffelwaffel mit Schokoladeneis und Vanillesauce

---

a starters
b main courses
c desserts
d lemon tart
e extra ingredients
f roast potatoes
g cinnamon
h chocolate ice cream

Pilzen (pl)	wild mushrooms
die Kartoffelpfanne	stir-fry potatoes
Champignons (pl)	button mushrooms
der Kartoffelpuffer	potato pancake

Hören

2 Hör zu. Was bestellt sie? (*What does she order?*)

> **Tipp**
> Remember the different ways to order food:
> *Ich möchte/Ich hätte gern...* (I'd like...)
> *Ich nehme...* (I'll take...)

Sprechen

3 Wählt ein Restaurant und bestellt etwas.

> Beispiel: Ich bin im „Kartoffelkeller". Als Vorspeise nehme ich...

5 Mahlzeit!

📖 Lesen

4 Lies die Restaurantbewertung (*restaurant reviews*) und finde die passenden Restaurants (1–3) aus Aktivität 1.

⭐⭐⭐⭐⭐ Bewertung am 12. Mai
Wirklich toll!
Die Atmosphäre ist herzlich, die Bedienung ist freundlich. Die Pommes sind klasse! Ich habe die Kartoffelpfanne „Mumbai" gegessen und Saft getrunken.
Tolles Konzept.
Heiko, Ellmau, Österreich

⭐⭐⭐⭐ Bewertung am 10. Oktober
Genial!
Ich habe eine Pizza Tonno mit Oliven gegessen und ich habe Cola getrunken.
Der Preis war gut und es war so lecker! Genial!
Sascha, Halle, Deutschland

⭐⭐⭐⭐ Bewertung am 5. Januar
Einfach aber gut
Die Atmosphäre ist ungemütlich, aber die Bedienung ist ziemlich freundlich. Ich habe Salat gegessen und dann Schnitzel. Ich habe Wasser getrunken. Es hat geschmeckt. Sehr einfach aber gut.
Aleks, Magdeburg, Deutschland

5 Lies die Restaurantbewertungen noch einmal. Finde die passenden Sätze (a–f) auf Deutsch.

a The atmosphere is warm.
b Great concept.
c The price was good and it was so delicious!
d The atmosphere is uncomfortable.
e The service is fairly friendly.
f Very simple but good.

Aa Grammatik p.111; WB p.59

The perfect tense with *haben*

The perfect tense is the most common past tense in German. It's formed using the present tense of *haben* or *sein* plus the past participle of the main verb (which can usually be recognised by the prefix *ge-*).

- *Ich esse die Kartoffelpfanne.* → *Ich **habe** die Kartoffelpfanne **gegessen**.*
- *Ich trinke Cola.* → *Ich **habe** Cola **getrunken**.*
- *Es schmeckt.* → *Es **hat geschmeckt**.*

🎧 Hören

6 🎵 Listen to Sven's restaurant review. Complete the sentences in English.

a The service at the 'Soup Temple' is _____.
b Sven ate _____.
c He drank _____.
d The atmosphere is _____.
e The price was _____.

⚙ Strategie

Using German creatively

The skills you use to write creatively in English can also be used in German.

- Look at other examples of the type of text you're writing, then decide what you could change.
- Use your imagination: which unexpected foods could your restaurant serve?
- Find ways to inject feeling into your work: *gar nicht* adds more emphasis than *nicht*, while intensifiers such as *sehr* and *wirklich* add impact.
- Take opportunities to broaden your vocabulary. An unusual word can make a big difference, but make sure you use it correctly.

✏ Schreiben

7 Schreib eine positive oder negative Restaurantbewertung. Das kann wahr oder erfunden sein. (*It can be real or made up.*)

Die Atmosphäre Die Bedienung	ist (gar nicht)	herzlich/toll/freundlich. ungemütlich/unfreundlich.
Ich habe	Suppe/Pommes/Pizza	gegessen.
	Cola/Wasser/Limonade	getrunken.
Es hat (nicht) geschmeckt.		

hundertfünf 105

5.5 Besser essen

Objectives
- Talking about healthy eating
- Using *man soll*
- Reading authentic texts

📖 Lesen

1 Was passt zusammen? Verbinde die Sätze (1–8) mit den Übersetzungen (a–h).

1. Man soll täglich gesund essen und trinken.
2. Man soll vegan oder vegetarisch essen.
3. Man soll regelmäßig viel Obst und Gemüse essen.
4. Man soll viel Wasser trinken.
5. Man soll wenig Fleisch essen.
6. Man soll wenig Fett essen.
7. Man soll wenig Zucker essen.
8. Man soll keine süßen Getränke trinken.

a. You should eat little meat.
b. You should eat a vegan or vegetarian diet.
c. You should eat little fat.
d. You should eat little sugar.
e. You shouldn't drink sugary drinks.
f. You should regularly eat lots of fruit and vegetables.
g. You should drink lots of water.
h. You should eat and drink healthily every day.

🔄 Übersetzen

2 Übersetz die Sätze ins Deutsche.

a. You should eat vegetables daily.
b. You should regularly drink water.
c. You shouldn't eat a lot of sugar.
d. You should eat a lot of fruit.

Aa Grammatik   p.111; WB p.61

Using *man soll*

In Unit 4, you encountered modal verbs in the form of *man muss* (to express what you <u>must</u> do), *man kann* (to express what you <u>can</u> do) and *man darf* (to express what you <u>are allowed to</u> do). Another modal verb expression is *man soll* (to express what you <u>should</u> do).

Man soll gesund essen. (You should eat healthily.)

As with other modal verbs, the second verb goes to the <u>end</u> of the sentence.

🎧 Hören

3 Hör zu. Ist das ein guter Tipp (GT) oder ein schlechter Tipp (ST) (1–4)?

💬 Sprechen

4 „Wie kann man besser essen?" Macht Dialoge.

Beispiel:
- Was soll man täglich essen?
- Man soll täglich Obst essen. Was soll man selten trinken?

Was soll man	täglich regelmäßig selten nie	essen? trinken?	
Man soll		Obst/Gemüse/Pommes/Käse/Schokolade	essen.
		Cola/Wasser/Tee/Kaffee	trinken.

5 Mahlzeit!

📖 **Lesen**

5 Lies den Artikel und finde die passenden Ausdrücke (a–f) auf Deutsch.

Ausgewogenes Essen für Kinder

„Das mag ich nicht." „Ich hab keinen Hunger." „Ich möchte Schokolade." Das hört man oft, aber eine ausgewogene Ernährung ist wichtig für Kinder!

Kinder sind meistens sehr aktiv und brauchen täglich Energie. Kohlenhydrate gibt es in vielen Formen: Brot, Kartoffeln, Nudeln, Reis.

Schnelle Energie hat man von Obst. In Äpfeln, Beeren und Pflaumen findet man Fruchtzucker.

Auch Fett gibt Energie. Einige pflanzliche Fette sind gute Fette: Sonnenblumenkerne zum Beispiel. Vitamine und Mineralstoffe sind auch wichtig.

Milchprodukte brauchen Kinder, denn sie müssen Kalzium haben. Mineralwasser ist auch ideal, weil es so gesund ist.

Beeren (pl)	berries
pflanzliche Fette (pl)	vegetable-/plant-based fats
Sonnenblumenkerne (pl)	sunflower seeds

a a balanced diet
b children are mostly very active
c carbohydrates
d fast energy
e vitamins and minerals
f dairy products

6 Read the article again and answer the questions in English.

a What do children often ask for?
b Which **four** sources of carbohydrate are mentioned in the text?
c Where can fructose be found?
d Which example of 'good fat' is given?
e Why do children need milk products?

⚙️ **Strategie**

Reading authentic texts

Reading authentic material can be daunting, but there are helpful questions you can ask yourself:

- What kind of text is it: magazine article, news report, story?
- What information would you expect to find in this kind of text?
- Which structures is the writer using: modal verbs to give advice, the perfect tense to narrate past events?

The more you read, the easier it becomes!

✏️ **Schreiben**

7 Isst du gesund? Schreib vier Sätze.

Beispiel:
Ich esse ziemlich gesund, denn ich esse...
Ich esse täglich/regelmäßig/nie...
Ich soll viel/wenig... essen.

5 Kultur

Eine kulinarische Reise

1. Spätzle
2. Wiener Schnitzel
3. Königsberger Klopse
4. Käsefondue
5. Maultaschen
6. Linzer Torte
7. Käsknöpfle
8. Soljanka
9. Kartoffelrösti
10. Marzipan
11. Sauerbraten
12. Buchweizentorte

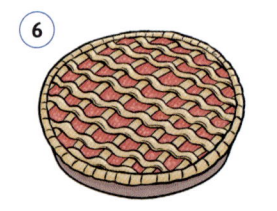

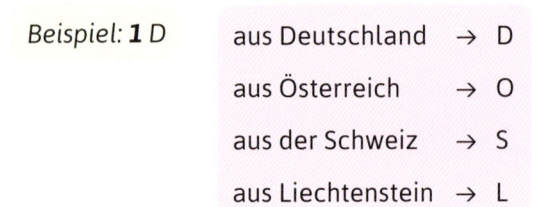

🎧 Hören

1 Hör zu. Woher kommen die Gerichte (1–12)? Schreib D, O, S oder L.

Beispiel: **1** D

aus Deutschland →	D
aus Österreich →	O
aus der Schweiz →	S
aus Liechtenstein →	L

📖 Lesen

2 Was ist das? Finde die passenden Bilder (1–12).

Beispiel: **1** k

a Eine Torte mit Marmelade und einem Gitter.
b Süß, aus Mandeln und Zucker. Das findet man in verschiedenen Formen und Farben.
c Ein Kuchen mit Preiselbeerkonfitüre und Sahne.
d Ein Gericht aus geschmolzenem Käse.
e Eine Suppe aus Fleisch, Tomaten, Paprika und Gewürzgurken.
f Eine Art Eiernudeln aus Liechtenstein.
g Hackfleisch-Bällchen mit einer weißen Soße mit Kapern.
h Quadratische Nudeltaschen mit Fleischfüllung.
i Dünn geschnittene Fleischstücke.
j Rindfleisch in Wein, Zwiebel und Karotten mariniert.
k Schwäbische Eiernudeln.
l Knusprige, gebratene Kartoffeln.

das Gitter	lattice	Hackfleisch-Bällchen (pl)	meatballs
Mandeln (pl)	almonds	dünn geschnitten	thinly sliced
der Kuchen	cake	das Rindfleisch	beef
die Sahne	cream	knusprig	crispy
geschmolzen	melted	gebraten	fried

5 Mahlzeit!

Hören

3 Hör zu und lies.

Die liebsten Traditionen in Deutschland, Österreich und der Schweiz

Deutschland – Kaffee und Kuchen

Kaffee und Kuchen ist eine deutsche Tradition, vor allem sonntags. Das ist eine traditionelle Mahlzeit zwischen Mittagessen und Abendessen.

Käsekuchen, Marmorkuchen in Gugelhupf-Form, Apfelkuchen, Schwarzwälder Kirschtorte. Man sitzt und redet und isst!

Österreich – Die Wiener Kaffeehauskultur

Das Kaffeehaus ist eine Institution in Wien. Früher haben Schriftsteller viele Stunden in diesen Kaffeehäusern verbracht. Komponisten wie Strauss, Mozart und Beethoven haben dort auch gespielt. „Café Sacher", „Café Dommayer", „Café Central", …

Trüffel-Torte, Zitronen-Torte, Himbeer-Torte, Mango-Schokoladen-Torte. Was isst du zu deinem Kaffee?

Schweiz – Das perfekte Fondue

In der Schweiz macht man das perfekte Käsefondue. Man muss Gruyere und Vacherin, Emmentaler und Appenzeller nehmen. Der Käse muss gut schmelzen. Dann braucht man Wein und Gewürze dazu. Cremig und lecker! Brot eintauchen macht Spaß!

Marmorkuchen	marble cake
Schwarzwälder Kirschtorte	black forest gâteau
man redet	people talk/chat
schmelzen	to melt
Gewürze (pl)	herbs and spices
eintauchen	to dip in

Lesen

4 Read the text again and complete the sentences in English.

a 'Coffee and cake' is enjoyed between _____ and _____ , mainly on _____ .
b Two cakes mentioned are _____ and _____ .
c Coffee houses are an important part of life in _____ .
d In Austria, writers and composers worked in _____ .
e For perfect fondue, the cheese has to _____ well.
f Dipping bread in the fondue is _____ .

Extra

Can you use the German you know to explain the following British dishes to someone who hasn't tried them?

- fish and chips
- apple tart
- bangers and mash
- toad in the hole
- bread and butter pudding

Sprechen

5 Macht drei Dialoge in der Eisdiele. Wähl von der Eiskarte.

Beispiel:
- Hallo, was darf es sein?
- Ich hätte gern eine Kugel Schokoeis.
- Sonst noch was?
- Eine Kugel…

Eiskarte

1 Kugel Eis		1,80 €
3 Kugeln Eis	ohne Sahne	4,80 €
	mit Sahne	5,90 €

Eissorten: Schokoeis, Himbeereis, Vanilleeis, Erdbeereis, Zitroneneis

hundertneun

5 Sprachlabor

The present tense of *essen* and *trinken*

Both *essen* and *trinken* take the same endings in the present tense:

ich _____e	wir _____en
du _____st	ihr _____t
er/sie/es _____t	sie/Sie _____en

However, while for *trinken* the stem (*trink-*) is used in all cases, for *essen* there is a vowel change for the *du* and *er/sie/es* forms, changing *ess-* to *iss-*. This is because *essen* is an irregular verb. You will need to learn these forms by heart.

1 Choose the correct form of *essen* or *trinken* to complete each sentence.

a Ich **esse/isst/essen** jeden Tag Haferflocken.
b Mein Bruder **esse/isst/esst** am Abend eine Portion Nudeln mit Hackfleischsoße.
c Meine Eltern **trinke/trinkt/trinken** selten Wein.
d Es ist gesünder, wenn man weniger süße Speisen **esse/isst/esst**.
e Herr Clausen, **isst/esst/essen** Sie oft im Restaurant?
f Pia, du **trinkst/trinkt/trinke** nicht genug Wasser. Das ist nicht gut.

2 Complete the sentences with the correct form of *essen*.

a Zum Frühstück _____ ich normalerweise Brot und Schinken.
b Was _____ ihr am Abend, Frank und Lutz?
c Maja und Ines _____ ihr zweites Frühstück um halb elf.
d _____ Sie gern Fastfood?
e Du _____ zu viele Kekse.
f Anna _____ viel Obst und Gemüse, denn das ist sehr gesund.

Using *ich möchte* and *ich hätte gern*

You use *ich möchte* and *ich hätte gern* to express that you would like something. These expressions are interchangeable. When the noun that follows is masculine, you change *ein* to *einen*. This is because the noun is a direct object in the accusative case and this affects the ending of masculine articles.

Ich möchte	ein**en** Flammkuchen. (masculine)
Ich hätte gern	eine Bratwurst. (feminine)
	ein Schinkenbrötchen. (neuter)

3 Divide each chain of letters into separate words and write the sentences.

a IchmöchteeinenKartoffelsalatund ichhättegerneinePizza.
b IchhättegerneineBratwurstundich möchteeineCola.
c IchmöchteeinenSalatmitOlivenundich hättegerneinMineralwassermitZitrone.

4 Complete the sentences with *einen*, *eine* or *ein*.

a Ich möchte als Nachspeise _____ Erdbeerkuchen. (m)
b Ich hätte gern _____ Limonade. (f)
c Und ich möchte _____ Nudelsuppe als Vorspeise. (f)
d Ich hätte gern als Hauptspeise _____ Hähnchen. (n)
e Ich möchte auch _____ Currywurst. (f)
f Ich hätte gern _____ Kartoffelknödel. (m)

5 Mahlzeit!

Starting to use the perfect tense with *haben*

The perfect tense is formed using the present tense of *haben* or *sein* plus the past participle of the main verb (which can usually be recognised by the prefix *ge-*). The past participle goes to the end of the sentence.

The verbs *essen* and *trinken* both take the perfect tense with *haben*.
- Ich **habe** Pizza **gegessen**. (I ate pizza.)
- Ich **habe** Cola **getrunken**. (I drank cola.)

Remember to change the form of *haben* depending on the person.
- Er **hat** Schokolade **gegessen**. (He ate chocolate.)
- Wir **haben** Kaffee **getrunken**. (We drank coffee.)

5 Look at the perfect tense burgers. Write sentences, putting a different word in the middle each time.

Example: **a** Ich habe <u>Tennis</u> gespielt.

a. Ich habe Basketball gespielt.
b. Ich habe Radio gehört.
c. Ich habe in Hamburg gewohnt.

6 Translate the sentences into German.

a. We ate bread and cheese.
b. Have you (*du*) eaten muesli?
c. He drank coffee.
d. Leon and Lorenz ate at half past nine.
e. I haven't eaten anything. ('*I've eaten nothing.*')

Using *sollen*

The verb *sollen* (should) is a modal verb. As with other modal verbs, you need to add a second verb to the sentence. This goes to the end and is in the infinitive (*-en*).

ich soll	I should
du sollst	you should
er/sie/es/man soll	he/she/it/one should
wir sollen	we should
ihr sollt	you should (plural)
sie/Sie sollen	you should (formal)

- Man **soll** jeden Tag Gemüse **essen**.
- Wir **sollen** mehr Wasser **trinken**.

7 Put the words in the correct order.

a. Man / trinken / soll / zwei Liter / Wasser.
b. soll / Er / essen / Obst und Gemüse.
c. soll / Cola / trinken / nicht / so / Man / viel.
d. weniger / Sie / sollen / Schokolade / essen.
e. Wir / organische Produkte / sollen / kaufen.
f. nicht / sollst / gehen / Du / so oft / in Fastfood Restaurants.

Aussprache: *ch* and *sch*

The German 'sch' sound is just like the English 'sh'. The German 'ch' sound is pronounced in two ways: after 'a', 'o' and 'u', it is like the 'ch' in 'Loch Ness'; after other vowels and consonants, it sounds like the 'h' sound in the English word 'huge'.

8 Listen and repeat. Then practise with your partner.

sprechen   österreichisch   Brötchen

Fleisch   Fisch   Milch   danach   noch

9 Practise saying the tongue twister.

Michael macht manchmal fantastische Schwarzwälder Kirschtorte.

hundertelf 111

5 Was kann ich schon?

📖 Lesen

1 Read Anna's blog post. Are the statements true (T) or false (F)?

> Hallo, ich bin die Anna. Für mich ist Essen total wichtig. <u>Ich esse gern internationales Essen, zum Beispiel italienisches, spanisches oder indisches Essen.</u>
>
> <u>Zum Frühstück esse ich eine Scheibe Brot und Schinken aber keinen Käse.</u> Dazu trinke ich schwarzen Tee. Meine Schwester trinkt lieber Früchtetee. Wenn ich nach Hause komme, sind meine Mutter und Vater nicht zu Hause und ich koche immer für mich und meine Schwester. Ich möchte gesünder kochen und mehr Gemüse essen, aber meistens mache ich nur Pizza und Pommes.
>
> Am Nachmittag esse ich dann meistens einen Snack aber nie Schokolade, weil sie zu zuckerhaltig ist. Mein Lieblingsessen sind Beeren, also esse ich Erdbeeren oder Himbeeren. Und zu Abend? Da gibt es immer eine kleine Mahlzeit. Vielleicht einen Joghurt oder manchmal Gemüsesuppe.

a Food is really important to Anna.
b She likes international food.
c For breakfast, she normally has a slice of bread, ham and cheese.
d She and her sister have black tea for breakfast.
e Anna's parents are not there when she gets home.
f She always cooks healthy food.
g She always has chocolate in the afternoon.
h She often has strawberries and raspberries.
i She has a big meal in the evening.
j She sometimes has vegetable soup in the evening. ✓ 10

2 Translate the <u>underlined</u> sentences from activity 1 into English. ✓ 10

Max. ✓ 20 Punkte

🎧 Hören

3 〰️ Listen. What food and drink does each person (1–5) order? Copy and complete the table with **exactly** what each person wants in English.

	Food	Drink
1		
2		

✓ 10

4 〰️ Listen to Bernd talking about his and his family's eating habits. Answer the questions in English.

a What does Bernd eat for breakfast? (**two** details)
b What does he drink for breakfast?
c What does Bernd's brother eat for breakfast?
d What does Bernd think about it?
e Which **two** food items does Bernd mention he eats for lunch?
f Why does he eat these two items?
g Where does he sometimes go in the afternoon?
h What is his favourite ice cream flavour?

✓ 10

Max. ✓ 20 Punkte

5 Mahlzeit!

✏️ Schreiben

5 Korrigiere die Rechtschreibfehler (*spelling mistakes*).

a Shokolade (*chocolate*)
b Ries (*rice*)
c Hänchen (*chicken*)
d Gemuse (*vegetables*)
e Milsch (*milk*)
✓ 5

6 Bring die Wörter in die richtige Reihenfolge.

a Was / sein? / darf / es
b Ich / eine Tomatensuppe, / möchte / bitte.
c Und / was / Sie / zu trinken? / möchten
d ein Glas / Ich / nehme / Mineralwasser.
e esse / kein / Ich / Fleisch, / Vegetarier / bin. / weil / ich
f gern / Reis, / Ich / esse / lecker / ist. / weil / es
g isst / zum Mittagessen? / du / gern / Was
h essen. / soll / weniger / Man / Zucker
i sollen / Wir / viel / Obst und Gemüse / essen.
j lecker. / Schokolade / sehr gesund / ist / nicht / aber
✓ 10

7 Übersetz den Text ins Deutsche.

For breakfast I eat bread and jam. My favourite jam is strawberry jam. It is tasty. For lunch I eat chicken and rice. I also eat chocolate for lunch and dinner, but that is unhealthy.

✓ 5

Max. ✓ **20 Punkte**

Deine Resultate

How many points did you get?

Ask your teacher for the answers. Write down your score out of a total of 20 for Reading. Then do the same for Listening and Writing.

Find the right combination of Bronze, Silver and Gold activities for you on pp.114–115!

Up to 6 points Well done! Do the Bronze activity in the next section.

7–12 points Great! Do the Silver activity in the next section.

13–20 points Fantastic! Do the Gold activity in the next section.

hundertdreizehn

5 Vorankommen!

Bronze

1 📖 **Read Yvonne's message and answer the questions in English.**

> Hallo!
> Ich heiße Yvonne. Mein Lieblingshobby ist Backen. Ich finde Backen voll super. Ich mache jede Woche drei Kuchen. Mein Lieblingskuchen ist Käsekuchen. Ich finde Käsekuchen total lecker. Mein Bruder mag Käsekuchen nicht, aber er liebt Schokoladenkuchen. Er isst jeden Tag Schokoladenkuchen, aber zum Geburtstag mache ich immer einen Erdbeerkuchen mit viel Sahne für meinen Bruder. Meine Mutter findet, man soll nicht so viel Kuchen essen, weil es nicht gesund ist.

a How many cakes does Yvonne bake per week?
b What is her favourite cake?
c Which type of cake does Yvonne's brother love?
d How often does he eat cake?
e Which type of cake does Yvonne bake for her brother's birthday?
f What does their mother say about eating cake?

2 🎧 **Listen to the interviews. What food does each person (1–5) like 🙂 and dislike 😕? Copy and complete the table in English.**

	🙂	😕
1		
2		

3 ✏️ **Answer the questions in German.**

a Was isst du zum Frühstück?
b Was ist dein Lieblingsessen?
c Welchen Kuchen isst du am liebsten?
d Was isst du nicht gern?
e Was soll man oft essen?

Silber

4 📖 **Read the information about Tim Mälzer, a German TV chef. Are the statements true (T) or false (F)?**

Tim Mälzer ist ein deutscher Koch. Man kann Tim Mälzer oft im Fernsehen sehen. Er kann natürlich sehr gut kochen. Er kocht auch zu Hause. Zu Hause isst er mit seiner Familie oft Hähnchen und Gemüse. Tim Mälzer denkt, man soll mehr als ein Gericht machen. Wenn die Eltern zum Beispiel nur Pommes machen, dann essen die Kinder nur Pommes. Ein Tipp: Nudeln und Gemüse nicht mischen. Besser ist: Nudeln und Gemüse separat haben. Dann essen es die Kinder.

a Tim Mälzer is often on TV.
b He never cooks at home.
c They often have fish with vegetables at home.
d He thinks knowing how to cook one dish is enough.
e He thinks children learn from their parents.
f He says that mixing pasta and vegetables is the best way to get children to eat both.

5 🎧 **Listen to Dennis talking about his eating habits. Complete the sentences in English.**

1 For breakfast Dennis eats _____.
2 For breakfast he drinks _____.
3 His favourite food is _____.
4 He does not like eating _____.
5 He goes to a restaurant _____.
6 He thinks he should drink less _____.
7 He thinks he should eat more _____.
8 Overall, he thinks his diet is _____.

6 ✏️ **Schreib einen Dialog (40–60 Wörter) in einem Restaurant. Der Kellner/Die Kellnerin muss drei bis vier Sätze sagen und der Gast muss drei bis vier Sätze sagen.** Write a restaurant dialogue (40–60 words). The server and the customer must say three to four sentences each.

5 Mahlzeit!

Gold

7 **Lies Omers Blogeintrag und beantworte die Fragen auf Englisch.**

Omer
12 September

Ich finde Kochen und Backen voll klasse. Sie sind meine absoluten Lieblingshobbys.

Ich sehe jeden Tag Backshows im Fernsehen. Backshows gibt es in vielen Ländern. Man hat nur eine Stunde Zeit und man muss einen komplizierten Kuchen backen. Ich finde die Shows total spannend. Es ist auch manchmal lustig, wenn es Probleme gibt. Oft fällt ein Kuchen auf den Boden, oder der Ofen ist zu heiß und der Kuchen verbrennt.

Ich möchte in einer Backshow mitmachen. Warum? Erstens, weil ich Backen liebe, zweitens, weil der Gewinner zehntausend Euro gewinnt und drittens, weil ich ein Buch mit meinen Rezepten schreiben möchte.

der Boden	the floor
verbrennen	to burn

a What are Omer's two favourite hobbies?
b How often does he watch baking programmes?
c Where are baking programmes shown?
d Which reason does he give for liking the programmes?
e Give one example of what he finds funny about the programmes.
f Which three reasons does he give for wanting to be in a baking show himself?

8 **Hör zu. Ein Experte spricht über die richtige Ernährung für Hunde. Wähl die vier richtigen Sätze.**

a Feed a dog only once per day when it is six months old.
b Every dog needs to be fed twice a day.
c You should feed your dog at different times every day.
d It is ideal to feed your dog at midday.
e Food should be at room temperature.
f Give your dog regular snacks.
g Dogs should have one day a week without food.
h Dogs and cats can have the same food.

Leckereien (pl)	treats

9 **Übersetz die Sätze ins Deutsche.**

a We should eat more fruit.
b You (*man*) should eat more vegetables because it is healthy.
c For breakfast she drinks a cup of tea with milk or lemon.
d What do you (*du*) like eating?
e I would like tomato soup, please.
f I would like a litre of milk, please.

10 **Schreib einen Paragrafen (zirka 80 Wörter) über deine Ernährung.**

Schreib:

- was dein Lieblingsessen ist, und warum
- was du nicht gern isst, und warum
- was man essen und trinken soll, und warum.

🎁 Extra

Try to do some research on eating habits in German-speaking countries and write six to eight sentences about the information you find.

Beispiel: *In der Schweiz essen Jugendliche normalerweise…*

hundertfünfzehn

5 Vokabeln

🎵 5.1 Frühstück – die wichtigste Mahlzeit!
Breakfast – the most important meal!

Was isst du zum Frühstück?	What do you eat for breakfast?
Was trinkst du zum Frühstück?	What do you drink for breakfast?
Ich esse/trinke … mit…	I eat/drink … with…
Ich esse kein Frühstück.	I don't eat breakfast.

das Brot	bread
die Butter	butter
Frühstücksflocken (pl)	breakfast cereal
der Joghurt	yoghurt
der Kaffee	coffee
die Käse	cheese
Kekse (pl)	biscuits
die Marmelade	jam
die Milch	milk
das Müsli	muesli
das Obst	fruit
der Saft	juice
der Schinken	ham
der Tee	tea
das Wasser	water
die Wurst	sausage

das Frühstück	breakfast
das Mittagessen	lunch
das Abendessen	evening meal, dinner
zum Frühstück/Mittagessen/Abendessen	for breakfast/lunch/dinner

die Ernährung	diet, eating habits
das Fastfood	fast food
das Gemüse	vegetables
gesund	healthy
das Hähnchen	chicken
Kartoffeln (pl)	potatoes
Nüsse (pl)	nuts

🎵 5.2 Wie schmeckt's?
How does it taste?

Was nimmst du?	What are you having?/What will you have?
Ich nehme einen/eine/ein…	I'll take a…
Was kostet das?	What does that cost?
Es kostet … Euro/Cent.	It costs … euros/cent.

die Dose Cola/Limonade/Soda	can of cola/lemonade/fizzy drink
die Flasche Wasser	bottle of water
100 Gramm Butter	100 grams of butter
der Liter Milch/Saft	litre of milk/juice
die Packung Kekse	packet of biscuits
die Scheibe Schinken	slice of ham
das Stück Käse	piece of cheese
die Tafel Schokolade	bar of chocolate
die Tüte Gummibärchen	bag of gummy bears

schmecken	to taste good, to be tasty
Schmeckt's dir?/Schmeckt es dir?	Does that taste good?/Do you find it tasty?
Es schmeckt mir./Mir schmeckt's.	It tastes good.
…schmeckt mir (nicht).	(about food/drink) I (don't) like…

Eier (pl)	eggs
das Fleisch	meat
Nudeln (pl)	pasta
der Reis	rice
der Salat	salad
das Soda	fizzy drink
das Lieblingsessen	favourite food
das Lieblingsgetränk	favourite drink

5 Mahlzeit!

5.3 Foodtruck-Fieber!
Foodtruck fever!

Hast du Hunger?	Are you hungry?
Was darf es sein?	What would you like (to order/buy)?
Ich möchte/hätte gern einen/eine/ein...	(about food/drink) I would like a...
Etwas zu trinken?	(Would you like) anything to drink?
Sonst noch was?	(Can I get you) anything else?

die Bratwurst	sausage
das Brötchen	(bread) roll
der Flammkuchen	thin pizza
der Hamburger	burger
der Knödel	dumpling
die Pizza	pizza
Pommes (pl)	chips
die Suppe	soup

gesund essen	to eat healthily
Ich esse kein Fleisch/Fisch.	I don't eat meat/fish.
Ich esse alles.	I eat everything/anything.
Lecker!	Delicious!
der/die Vegetarier/Vegetarierin	vegetarian
der/die Veganer/Veganerin	vegan

5.4 Guten Appetit!
Enjoy your meal!

die Vorspeise	starter
das Hauptgericht	main course
die Nachspeise	dessert

das Eis	ice cream
das Omelett	omelette
die Sahne	cream
das Schnitzel	cutlet, escalope
die Torte	tart

die Atmosphäre	atmosphere
die Bedienung	service
der Preis	price
das Restaurant	restaurant
die Restaurantbewertung	restaurant review

herzlich	warm
klasse	great
ungemütlich	uncomfortable

5.5 Besser essen
Eating better

Man soll ... essen/trinken.	You ought to eat/drink...

nie	never
regelmäßig	regularly
selten	rarely
täglich	every day
viel	a lot of
wenig	little, a little of, not much

eine ausgewogene Ernährung	balanced diet
das Fett	fat
Kohlenhydrate (pl)	carbohydrates
Milchprodukte (pl)	dairy products
Mineralstoffe (pl)	minerals
süße Getränke (pl)	sugary drinks
Vitamine (pl)	vitamins
der Zucker	sugar

6 Die Welt des Lesens
Los geht's!

1 Wann hatten sie Geburtstag (a–f)? Such Informationen im Internet, dann verbinde die Autoren mit den richtigen Geburtsdaten.

Beispiel: **a** 10 Dezember 1958

Kultur

Germany is sometimes described as *das Land der Dichter und Denker* ('the land of poets and thinkers'). This nickname refers to the many famous German writers, composers, philosophers and scientists, such as Goethe and Schiller, Bach and Beethoven, Immanuel Kant and Albert Einstein. Famous German cultural figures who have been celebrated on banknotes include the Grimm brothers, mathematician Carl Gauss, scientists Paul Ehrlich and Maria Sibylla Merian, composer Clara Schumann, and the writers Bettina von Arnim and Annette von Droste-Hülshoff.

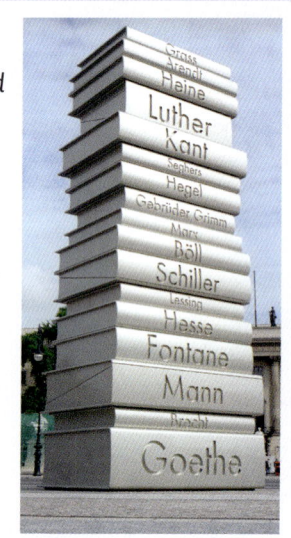

1700

28 August 1749

4 Januar 1785

1800

- a Cornelia Funke
- b Bernhard Schlink
- c Johann W. Goethe
- d Bertolt Brecht
- e Franz Kafka
- f Jacob Grimm

3 Juli 1883

1900

10 Februar 1898

6 Juli 1944

10 Dezember 1958

2000

6 Die Welt des Lesens

2 Lies die Meinungen über deutsche Literatur. Positiv (P), negativ (N) oder beides (P+N)?

Sprachmuster

In German, to indicate that something belongs to someone, we add the possessive -s: *Hannahs Buch, Goethes Faust*. An important difference to English is that German does not use an apostrophe before the s.

Leseratte Ich habe in der Schule Goethes *Faust* gelesen. Das war überhaupt nicht einfach, aber mit etwas Hilfe von unserem Lehrer konnte ich es verstehen. Faust war ganz interessant.

Literatur-Leo Wir haben in der Schule *Die Verwandlung* von Franz Kafka gelesen und das war so kompliziert! Das hat keinen Spaß gemacht.

Buchprinzessin Ich habe gerade *Tintenherz* von Cornelia Funke gelesen und kann das empfehlen. Es war total spannend und ich habe das ganze Buch in zwei Tagen gelesen.

Hannah_auf_der_Erbse Ich habe *Das Leben des Galilei*, ein Theaterstück von Brecht, gelesen. Manche Stellen waren langweilig, aber es hat mir gut gefallen.

3 Welche Märchen (fairy tales) hast du als Kind gern gelesen? Schreib Sätze.

- Schneewittchen und die sieben Zwerge
- Dornröschen
- Rotkäppchen
- Rumpelstilzchen
- Aschenputtel
- Hänsel und Gretel
- Der Wolf und die sieben Geißlein
- Die Bremer Stadtmusikanten
- Rapunzel
- Das tapfere Schneiderlein
- Schneeweißchen und Rosenrot

😢	traurig	sad
😆	lustig	funny
😱	gruselig	spooky/scary
😮	spannend	exciting
😜	albern	silly

Beispiel: Ich habe gern Rumpelstilzchen *gelesen.* Das war spannend. Aber ich habe nicht gern Hänsel und Gretel *gelesen.* Das war zu gruselig.

Kultur

The fairy tales written by the Brothers Grimm have been translated into more than 160 languages. Some of the most famous fairy tale characters were created by them. There were 50 tales, but some have gained much more fame than others.

4 Match the English literary terms (1–6) to the German definitions (a–f).

1. a play
2. a short story
3. a fairy tale
4. a novel
5. an author
6. a poem

a. Ein Märchen ist oft über Hexen, Prinzen und Prinzessinnen.
b. Ein Gedicht hat oft Reime (zum Beispiel, „Haus – Maus") und symbolische Wörter.
c. Ein Roman kann sehr lang sein.
d. Ein Theaterstück hat Dialoge und man kann es im Theater sehen.
e. Eine Kurzgeschichte ist nicht so lang wie ein Buch.
f. Ein Autor/Eine Autorin schreibt Bücher, Gedichte oder Theaterstücke.

hundertneunzehn

6.1 Berühmte Autoren

Objectives
- Getting to know German-speaking writers
- Revising the perfect tense with *haben*
- Researching German culture

✏️ Schreiben

1 Füll die Lücken aus.

gelebt   gewonnen   studiert   gegründet

gesammelt   geschrieben   gemacht

Jura	law
gegründet	founded, established (perfect tense of *gründen*)
gesammelt	collected (perfect tense of *sammeln*)

a Cornelia Funke hat aus ihrem Buch *Tintenherz* einen Film _____ .
b Hermann Hesse hat 1946 den Nobelpreis für Literatur _____ .
c Bernhard Schlink hat Jura _____ .
d Johann W. Goethe hat in Weimar _____ .
e Bertolt Brecht hat 1949 eine Theatergruppe _____ .
f Die Brüder Grimm haben viele Märchen _____ .
g Rainer Maria Rilke hat Gedichte auf Deutsch und Französisch _____ .

🎧 Hören

2 Listen to Jan's presentation about Erich Kästner and answer the questions in English.

a Which country was Erich Kästner from?
b Where was he born?
c What did he study?
d Besides poetry, what else did he write?
e Which three facts reflect his success and fame?

3 Lies die *Grammatik*. Dann hör Jans Präsentation noch einmal zu und schreib die sechs Partizipien (*past participles*) auf.

Beispiel: gelebt, …

Aa Grammatik   p.126; WB p.63

The perfect tense with *haben* (revision)

The perfect tense needs two parts: an auxiliary verb (e.g. *haben*) and the past participle. The past participle usually starts with *ge-*, but sometimes this is not added, for example when the verb already begins with *ge-* (*gewinnen* → *gewonnen*), when it begins with a prefix such as *be-*, *ver-* or *miss-* (*verstehen* → *verstanden*) or when it ends in *-ieren* (*studieren* → *studiert*).

Remember that the auxiliary verb changes depending on the person of the verb (*ich*, *du*, etc.) but the past participle never changes.

Ich **habe** viele Gedichte von Goethe **gelesen**.

Goethe **hat** den Faust **geschrieben**.

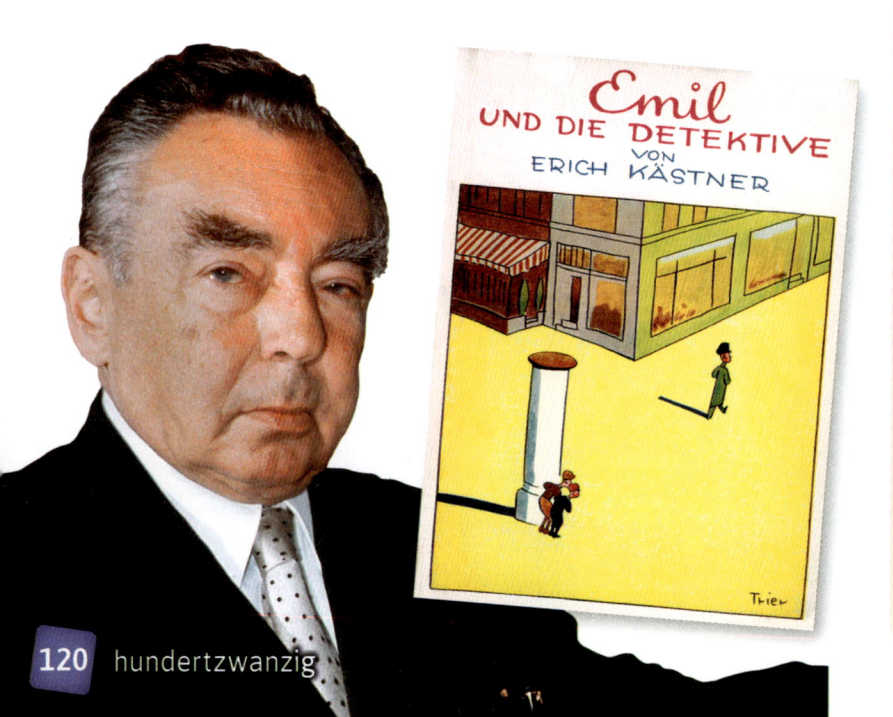

6 Die Welt des Lesens

💬 Sprechen

4 👥 Du bist ein berühmter Autor/eine berühmte Autorin. Mach Dialoge mit deinem Partner/deiner Partnerin. Stellt und beantwortet die Fragen mit den Informationen.

- Wann hast du gelebt?
- Wo hast du gewohnt?
- Was hast du studiert?
- Welche Werke hast du geschrieben?
- In welchen Genres hast du geschrieben?

Ingeborg Bachmann
1926–1973

Wohnort: Wien
Studium: Psychologie, Philosophie
bekannte Werke: *Malina*, *Simultan*
Genre: Kurzgeschichten, Gedichte, Briefe

Franz Kafka
1883–1924

Wohnort: Prag
Studium: Jura
bekannte Werke: *Die Verwandlung*, *Das Urteil*
Genre: Romane, Kurzgeschichten, Briefe

✏️ Schreiben

5 Schreib eine kurze Biographie mit der Information aus Aktivität 4.

Ich habe Er/Sie hat	von … bis … gelebt.
	in … gelebt/gewohnt.
	…studiert.
	…geschrieben.

⚙️ Strategie

Researching German culture

Use the internet to research, but try not to rely on one source only. Be aware that online encyclopedias are not necessarily written by professionals! When exploring other cultures, have fun with it and look for areas that interest you personally. Apart from facts, you can also find great video clips about many famous German poems and books.

🔄 Übersetzen

6 Übersetz den Text über Horst Eckert (Janosch) ins Deutsche.

> My favourite author is Horst Eckert. He lived in Poland and Germany, but today he lives in Tenerife. He studied art in Munich. He wrote more than 150 children's books. My favourite book is called *Oh, wie schön ist Panama*.

✏️ Schreiben

7 Such Informationen im Internet über einen Autor/eine Autorin aus Deutschland, Österreich oder der Schweiz. Mach ein Poster mit vier Fakten in der 'er'/'sie'-Form.

Beispiel: Cornelia Funke ist eine beliebte deutsche Autorin. Sie hat in Dorsten gewohnt. Sie hat…

⚠️ Achtung!

When you translate a text containing place names, remember to check whether these are the same in German or not.

💡 Tipp

You could research a famous author of a classic work of literature or one of the authors mentioned in activity 1. Alternatively, find out about a successful 21st century writer, such as Daniel Kehlmann, Julia Franck, Sibylle Berg, Herta Müller or Wolfgang Herrndorf.

hunderteinundzwanzig

6.2 Es war einmal…

Objectives
- Learning about the German fairy tale tradition
- Starting to use the imperfect tense
- Practising creative writing

Lesen

1 Read the descriptions of well-known fairy tales. What are their titles in English?

a Die Großmutter war krank im Bett und wohnte in einem Haus im Wald.
b Das Mädchen hatte lange blonde Haare und wohnte in einem hohen Turm.
c Aschenputtel hatte zwei böse und faule Stiefschwestern.
d Die böse Stiefmutter hatte einen Spiegel, der sprechen konnte.
e Die Prinzessin war in einem hundertjährigen Schlaf.
f Die beiden Kinder waren im Wald und kamen zu einem Lebkuchenhaus von einer Hexe.

2 Finde die passenden Wörter (a–f) auf Deutsch aus Aktivität 1.

a forest
b tower
c mirror
d sleep (*noun*)
e gingerbread house
f witch

Hören

3 Hör zu und füll die Lücken aus.

Es war einmal eine **1** _____, sie hieß Schneewittchen. Sie war sehr schön und hatte lange schwarze Haare. Sie lebte in einem Schloss mit ihrem Vater und ihrer **2** _____, aber die Stiefmutter war sehr böse und neidisch. Die Stiefmutter wollte Schneewittchen töten, deshalb wohnte Schneewittchen mit den **3** _____ Zwergen in einem kleinen Haus im **4** _____. Die Zwerge und die Tiere im Wald waren ihre Freunde. Eines Tages aber kam die Stiefmutter zum Haus und gab Schneewittchen einen vergifteten **5** _____. Schneewittchen war wie tot und die Zwerge waren sehr traurig. Da kam ein Prinz auf einem **6** _____ und küsste Schneewittchen. Schneewittchen und der Prinz waren für immer glücklich.

es war einmal	once upon a time
töten	to kill
vergiftet	poisoned
tot	dead
glücklich	happy

Grammatik p.126; WB p.65

The imperfect tense

The imperfect tense is used more in written than in spoken German. However, the verbs *haben* and *sein* are very commonly used in this tense in speech as well, instead of in the perfect tense.

ich	hatte	war
du	hattest	warst
er/sie/es	hatte	war
wir	hatten	waren
ihr	hattet	wart
sie/Sie	hatten	waren

Note that the *ich* and *er/sie/es* forms have the same verb form.

Lesen

4 Was passt zusammen?

1 wohnte
2 hieß
3 gab
4 wollte
5 kam
6 küsste

a wanted
b gave
c lived
d was called
e kissed
f came

6 Die Welt des Lesens

🎧 Hören

5 Listen to Svenja's podcast about fairy tales. Complete the sentences in English.

a I find most fairy tales _____.
b I find it boring that the _____ always needs help.
c *The Brave Little Tailor* is Svenja's _____ fairy tale.
d In this story there are no _____.
e The tailor is _____ and very _____.
f One afternoon he kills _____ flies and declares himself a hero.

✏️ Schreiben

6 Erfinde den Anfang (*invent the beginning*) von einem Märchen. Schreib fünf bis acht Sätze.

Es war einmal	ein Mädchen/ein Junge. eine Prinzessin/ein Prinz. ein Wolf/eine Ziege/ ein Frosch/ein Monster.
Er/Sie war (sehr/ziemlich/ein bisschen)	groß/klein/reich/arm/schön/hässlich/lieb/böse/mutig.
Er/Sie hatte	lange/kurze Haare. blaue/grüne/braune Augen.
Er/Sie hatte	keine Geschwister. eine Schwester/einen Bruder. eine (böse) Stiefmutter/Stiefschwester. keine Eltern.
Er/Sie wohnte in	einem (kleinen) Haus/einem Schloss/einem Turm/einer Höhle.

💬 Sprechen

7 👥 Beschreib eine Märchenfigur. Dein Partner/Deine Partnerin muss raten, wer das ist.

Beispiel: Wer ist das? Die Person hatte kurze schwarze Haare und war schlank. Er wohnte in Persien und hatte eine magische Lampe.

⚙️ Strategie

Practising creative writing

When writing in German, try to make the most of language you've learnt previously. In this unit, for example, you can draw on vocabulary for describing people. Your answers do not always need to be true – show off your creativity and your ability to use words in new ways. For example, you could write that Little Red Riding Hood was 13 years old – that might not be a fact, but it shows your ability to use previously learnt vocabulary and sentence structures.

🔄 Übersetzen

8 Translate the text into English.

Es war einmal ein Mädchen. Sie hieß Lena. Sie wohnte in einem kleinen Haus in Deutschland. Sie war nett und sehr musikalisch und sie hatte einen Traum: Eurovision zu gewinnen! Lena war sehr mutig und am Ende hatte sie viele Fans in Deutschland und auf der ganzen Welt.

✏️ Schreiben

9 Denk an eine berühmte Person und schreib ein kurzes Märchen über sein/ihr Leben. Benutz den Text aus Aktivität 8 zur Hilfe.

hundertdreiundzwanzig

6 Kultur

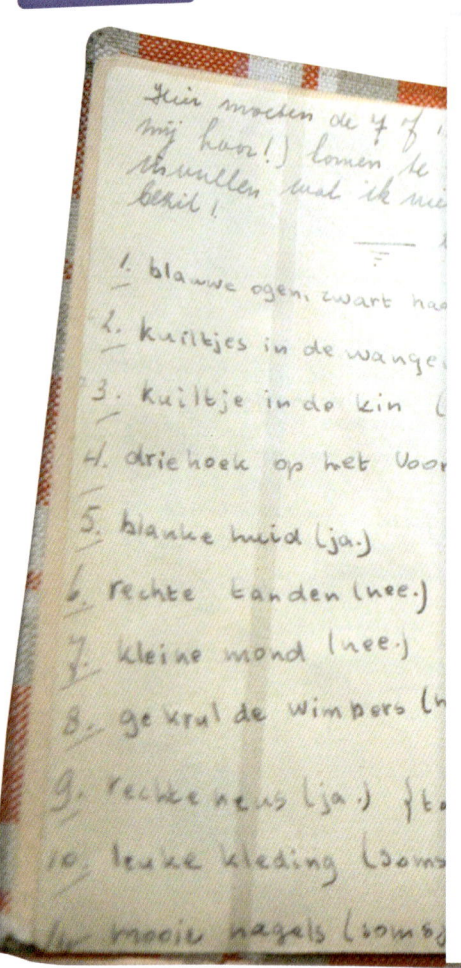

Das Leben der Anne Frank

Anne Franks Tagebuch

Das Buch beginnt am 12. Juni 1942. An diesem Tag hat Anne Frank Geburtstag, es ist ihr dreizehnter Geburtstag. Zum Geburtstag bekommt sie ein Tagebuch und Spiele. Ihre Mutter backt ihr einen Erdbeerkuchen. Dann hat sie eine Geburtstagsfeier mit ihren Freunden.

In ihrem Tagebuch erzählt Anne Frank über ihr Leben, ihre Schule, ihre Freunde, Jungen (die in sie verliebt sind) und ihre Familie. Sie hat am Anfang ein ziemlich normales Leben. Dann gibt es viele Regeln für jüdische Menschen wie die Familie Frank, zum Beispiel müssen sie einen gelben Stern tragen.

Am 8. Juli 1942 schreibt sie, wie sie sich vor der SS verstecken müssen. Das Versteck ist das Hinterhaus am alten Arbeitsplatz des Vaters. Sie müssen immer leise sein und Anne hat große Angst, dass die Nazis sie finden. Die Familie Van Daan wohnt mit Annes Familie in dem Versteck. Viele von Annes Geschichten im Tagebuch erzählen über das tägliche Leben, ihre Familie und manchmal über politische Ereignisse.

Am 1. August 1944 schreibt Anne zum letzten Mal in ihr Tagebuch. Sie hofft, dass Hitler stirbt und dass der Krieg zu Ende geht.

erzählt über	talks about
verliebt	in love
die SS (Schutzstaffel)	a special police force under Hitler
der Stern	star
leise	quiet
Ereignisse (pl)	events
stirbt	dies
der Krieg	war

📖 Lesen

1 Lies den Text und finde die passenden Wörter (a–h) auf Deutsch.

a diary
b boys
c rules
d Jewish people
e to hide
f the hiding place
g fear
h she hopes

2 Read the text again and answer the questions in English.

a How old was Anne at the beginning of the book?
b What did she receive for her birthday?
c Why did Anne's life change?
d What happened in July 1942?
e What was Anne scared of?
f When was her last diary entry?

6 Die Welt des Lesens

🎧 Hören

3 Hör zu. Füll die Lücken aus.

Sie hieß Anne Frank. Ihr Geburtstag war der
1 _____ Juni. Sie hatte **2** _____
Haare und **3** _____ Augen. Sie hatte eine
Schwester, Margot. Sie hatte auch eine
4 _____, Moortje. Sie war Jüdin und
wohnte in einem Versteck in **5** _____.
Sie war sehr **6** _____ und **7** _____.
Sie liebte **8** _____ und schrieb
9 _____ in ihrem Tagebuch. Das
Tagebuch war ihre **10** _____ und hieß Kitty.

💡 Tipp
You can find Anne Frank's diary and more about her story online. Her family's original hiding place is now a museum in Amsterdam. The museum website offers a virtual tour through the rooms and gives more information about her life.

🔄 Übersetzen

4 Übersetz den Text über Anne Frank ins Deutsche.

Anne Frank came from Germany, but she also lived in Holland. There were (*Es gab...*) a lot of rules for Jewish people. She lived from 1942 to 1944 in a hiding place. Anne was intelligent and kind and she enjoyed writing. Anne's diary is so interesting. She talks about her family and friends and daily life. Her story is sad but also inspiring.

💬 Sprechen

5 👥 Macht ein Interview über das Leben der Anne Frank.

- Wofür ist Anne Frank bekannt?
- Wo hat Anne Frank gewohnt?
- Wie war sie? (zum Beispiel ihr Aussehen, ihre Persönlichkeit)
- Was wissen wir noch über ihr Leben und ihre Familie?

Under the Nazi regime, many authors were banned as they were considered to be against Hitler's ideas. On 10th May 1933, books by blacklisted authors were gathered together and burnt. The *Bibliothek* memorial in Berlin commemorates this event. It shows an underground library of empty bookshelves.

✏️ Schreiben

6 Schreib einen Tagebucheintrag über dein eigenes Leben (a *diary entry about your own life*). Du kannst über diese Punkte schreiben.

- Tagesroutine
- Familie
- Schule
- Essen
- Freunde

Um ... Uhr habe ich gelesen/Sport gemacht/Musik gehört.

Zu Mittag habe ich ... gegessen. Das war...

Mein Vater/Meine Mutter/Mein Bruder/Meine Schwester ist...

Mein Freund/Meine Freundin heißt... Er/Sie ist...

Mein Lieblingsfach ist... Mein Lehrer/Meine Lehrerin ist... Heute haben wir ... gelesen/geschrieben/gelernt.

hundertfünfundzwanzig

6 Sprachlabor

The perfect tense

The perfect tense consists of an auxiliary verb (*haben* or *sein*) and the past participle. The past participle usually starts with the prefix *ge-* and ends in either *-t* or *-en*. In general, *-t* is added to the stem of regular verbs and *-en* to the stem of irregular verbs. The past participle goes to the end of the clause.

For some irregular verbs, the vowel in the middle changes (*finden* → *gefunden*).

If the verb in the infinitive starts with *ge-*, you don't need to add another *-ge* (*gewinnen* → *gewonnen*).

Past participles of verbs ending in *-ieren*, as well as verbs that start with certain prefixes like *ver-* and *be-*, don't take *ge-* either (*verlieben* → *verliebt*, *besuchen* → *besucht*).

ich habe	getanzt
du hast	gehört
er/sie/es hat	gewohnt
wir haben	gelesen
ihr habt	geschrieben
sie/Sie haben	gesehen

1 Complete the text with the correct words.

gemacht   gelebt   Hast   komponiert

gelesen   haben   geschrieben   hat

Im Deutschunterricht **1** _____ wir *Wilhelm Tell* **2** _____ . Schiller hat dieses Drama 1804 **3** _____ . Man hat aus dem Theaterstück auch eine Oper und einen Film **4** _____ . Rossini hat die Musik für die Oper **5** _____ . **6** _____ du die *Wilhelm-Tell-Overtüre* gehört? Wilhelm Tell hat in der Schweiz **7** _____ . Man **8** _____ Wilhelm Tell als Helden gefeiert, weil er sehr mutig war.

The imperfect tense

The imperfect tense is a more formal past tense and is mainly used in writing. However, the imperfect forms of *haben* and *sein* are commonly used in spoken German as well, in place of the perfect tense.

	haben	sein	wohnen	kommen
ich	hat**te**	war	wohn**te**	kam
du	hat**test**	war**st**	wohn**test**	kam**st**
er/sie/es	hat**te**	war	wohn**te**	kam
wir	hat**ten**	war**en**	wohn**ten**	kam**en**
ihr	hat**tet**	war**t**	wohn**tet**	kam**t**
sie/Sie	hat**ten**	war**en**	wohn**ten**	kam**en**

2 Complete the text with the correct imperfect tense form of *haben*, *sein*, *wohnen* or *kommen*.

Schneewittchen **1** _____ sehr schön. Sie **2** _____ lange schwarze Haare. Sie **3** _____ zuerst in einem Schloss und dann in einem kleinen Haus mit den sieben Zwergen. Die Zwerge **4** _____ sieben kleine Betten in dem Haus. Alle Tiere im Wald **5** _____ Schneewittchens Freunde. Aber sie **6** _____ auch eine böse Stiefmutter. Die Stiefmutter **7** _____ sehr neidisch, weil Schneewittchen so gut aussehend war. Eines Tages **8** _____ die Stiefmutter mit einem vergifteten Apfel zum Haus der Zwerge…

Aussprache: pf

The 'pf' sound can come at the beginning, middle or end of a word. The trick is to run the two letters together very quickly to form one sound.

3 Practise saying the tongue twister.

Der tapfere Wilhelm Tell schießt einen Pfeil in den Apfel auf dem Kopf seines Sohnes.

6 Was kann ich schon?

6 Die Welt des Lesens

Die Bremer Stadtmusikanten

Es war einmal ein Esel, der wollte nach Bremen gehen, um Musik zu machen. Auf dem Weg nach Bremen hat er einen Hund, eine Katze und einen Hahn getroffen. Alle wollten ein neues Leben. Zusammen fanden sie in einem Haus Diebe. Die Tiere machten eine Pyramide vor dem Fenster. Unten war der Esel, auf ihm war der Hund, auf dem Hund war die Katze und auf der Katze war der Hahn. Dann begannen sie, Musik zu machen: IA, WAU WAU, MIAU, KIKERIKI! Die Diebe bekamen Angst und rannten aus dem Haus. Die vier tierischen Freunde wohnten dann zusammen in dem Haus.

der Esel	donkey
der Hahn	cockerel
Diebe (pl)	thieves
vor dem Fenster	in front of the window
rannten	ran (imperfect tense of *rennen*)

Lesen

1 Read the story of the *Town Musicians of Bremen* and answer the questions in English.

a What did the donkey want to do in Bremen?
b Who did he meet on the way?
c Who was in the house?
d Who stood on top of the dog?
e What did the thieves do when they got scared?

Hören

2 Hör zu. Wer sagt das: Yusuf (Y), Monika (M) oder Hannes (H)?

a Ich bin Fan von Erich Kästner.
b Ich mag keine Liebesgeschichten.
c Ich habe letzte Woche ein ganzes Buch gelesen.
d Ich interessiere mich für Kriegsgeschichten.
e Dramen finde ich besser als Gedichte.
f Wir lesen einen Roman von Bernhard Schlink im Deutschunterricht.

Schreiben

3 Lies die Informationen über den Autor Hermann Hesse. Schreib eine kurze Biographie (fünf bis sechs Sätze).

Hermann Hesse
1877–1962

Wohnort: Gaienhofen am Bodensee (Deutschland) und Montagnola (Schweiz)
Familie: drei Söhne
Genre: Kurzgeschichten und Gedichte
Bekannt für: 1946 Nobelpreis für Literatur

hundertsiebenundzwanzig

1 Sprungbrett

🎧 Hören

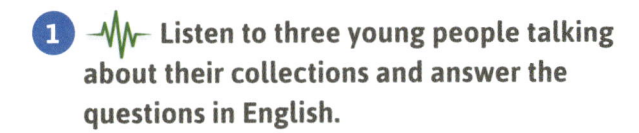

1 〰️ **Listen to three young people talking about their collections and answer the questions in English.**

Part 1:
a What is his name?
b Where does he live?
c What does he collect?

Part 2:
d How old is Sarah?
e What does she collect?
f How many of these does she have?

Part 3:
g What is his name?
h When did he start collecting?
i What does he collect?

> 💡 **Tipp**
> Dealing with unfamiliar language is an important listening skill. Don't panic if you encounter words you haven't read or heard before. The question wording can help you. For example, given that activity 1 is about collections and collecting, what could *Sammlung* and *ich sammle* mean?

2 〰️ **Listen to the description of Campino, the lead singer of *Die Toten Hosen*. Choose the <u>four</u> correct statements.**

a Campino's birthday is in June.
b He has lived in many different cities.
c He now lives in Cologne.
d Campino was born in 1962.
e He is in a punk rock band.
f He plays the guitar.
g He supports Liverpool FC.
h He is also famous for writing comic strips.

3 〰️ **Hör zu. Hassan, Olaf und Tanja sind Fußballfans. Sie sprechen über ihre Mannschaften und sich selbst.**

a	wohnt in Gelsenkirchen.
b	Lieblingsmannschaft ist Real Madrid.
c	hat am ersten April Geburtstag.
d	Lieblingsmannschaft ist FC Freiburg.
e	Lieblingsmannschaft ist FC Schalke.
f	wohnt in der Schweiz.

Schreib die richtigen Buchstaben in die Kästchen.

1 Hassan ☐ ☐
2 Olaf ☐ ☐
3 Tanja ☐ ☐

1 Hallo!

💬 Sprechen

4 Practise the role play.

Your teacher will play the part of your exchange partner and will speak first.

You should address your partner as *du*.

When you see this – ! – you will have to respond to something you have not prepared.

When you see this – ? – you will have to ask a question.

> Du sprichst mit deinem deutschen Austauschpartner/ deiner deutschen Austauschpartnerin über dich.
> - Name
> - Alter
> - !
> - Wohnort
> - ?

5 Practise the photo card activity.

Look at the photo and prepare notes to answer the following questions.

- Was gibt es auf dem Foto?
- Wann hast du Geburtstag?
- Wie findest du Geburtstagspartys?

Think about any other questions you may be asked in relation to **personal information**.

Your teacher will ask you the three questions and then **two more questions** which you have not prepared.

💡 Tipp

When your conversation skills are assessed, your teacher or examiner will be listening out for several things:

- **Communication and content:** what you say needs to be relevant, with as much detail as you can give.
- **Range and accuracy:** use more complex structures once you're confident you can use them without making mistakes.
- **Pronunciation and intonation:** take care with how you pronounce words. A good knowledge of sound-spelling links will help you avoid getting into bad habits.
- **Fluency:** being able to think on your feet and give spontaneous answers can be difficult early on, but as your knowledge of vocabulary and structures builds, it will get easier and easier. Listening to native speakers will also help.

6 Your teacher will ask you these questions. Answer them <u>without</u> making notes, using the language you already know.

- Wo wohnst du?
- Wie schreibt man das?
- Wie findest du deine Stadt/ dein Dorf?

2 Sprungbrett

Lesen

1 Read the passage and choose the correct answers.

Die beliebtesten Haustiere der Deutschen

Wir knuddeln unsere Katzen, tätscheln unsere Hunde und streicheln unsere Meerschweinchen.

Die Deutschen lieben ihre Haustiere. 38 Prozent der Deutschen besitzen ein Haustier. Bei Familien mit Kindern ist der Anteil höher: 57 Prozent.

Aber welches ist das beliebteste Haustier?

1 — Platz 1: Katzen
In deutschen Haushalten leben 11,8 Millionen Katzen. Sie haben oft eine Katzenklappe.

2 — Platz 2: Hunde
Der Hund ist der beste Freund des Menschen. Rund 6,8 Millionen Menschen haben einen Hund.

3 — Platz 3: Kleintiere
5,9 Millionen Kinder finden Hamster, Meerschweinchen und Kaninchen tolle Spielkameraden!

4 — Platz 4: Vögel
Vögel sind sehr beliebt. 4 Millionen haben Wellensittiche, Kanarienvögel oder Finken.

5 — Platz 5: Fische
2,1 Millionen haben in ihrem Zuhause ein Aquarium.

Tipp
Don't panic if there are words you don't know in this text. Use the questions to help you find the information you need.

1 What percentage of German households with children have a pet?
   a 38
   b 57
   c 48
2 What is the most popular pet?
   a fish
   b cats
   c rabbits
3 How are dogs described?
   a man's best friend
   b their own best friend
   c a cat's best friend
4 Which small animals are not mentioned in third place?
   a mice
   b hamsters
   c rabbits
5 How many people have birds?
   a 5 million
   b 4 million
   c 3 million
6 What do 2.1 million people have at home?
   a a rabbit hutch
   b an aquarium
   c a cat flap

2 Das ist meine Welt!

2 Lies das Poster. Beantworte die Fragen auf Deutsch.

Café Katzenparadies

Sechs Katzen wohnen in einer stressfreien Atmosphäre in diesem Kaffeehaus.

Sie heißen: Felix, Susi, Momo, Lara, Moritz und Bennie.

Sonntags um 16 Uhr gibt es Jazzmusik.

Adresse:
Wilhelminastraße 131
10585 Berlin

Öffnungszeiten:
Dienstag bis Sonntag
10–19 Uhr

- a Wo ist das Katzencafé?
- b Wie ist die Atmosphäre im Café?
- c Wie heißen die Katzen?
- d Wann gibt es Live-Musik?
- e Wann ist das Café geschlossen (*closed*)?

3 Translate the sentences into English.

- a Ich bin freundlich und auch lustig.
- b Ich habe zwei Schwestern und einen Stiefbruder.
- c Ich habe drei Meerschweinchen und zwei Hunde.
- d Ich habe kurze blonde Haare.
- e Ich habe am zehnten August Geburtstag.

Tipp
Remember that German phrases cannot always be translated word for word into English.

Ich habe am … Geburtstag. = ~~I have on … birthday.~~
My birthday is on…

Schreiben

4 Du schickst dieses Foto an eine deutsche Freundin. Schreib **vier** Sätze auf Deutsch über das Foto.

- Auf dem Foto sehe ich… (ein Mädchen/ einen Jungen/eine Familie).
- Der Junge ist/hat…
- Das Mädchen ist/hat…

Tipp
- Use the sentence starters above to help you structure your sentences.
- Go with what you know how to say: how old is each person? What do they look like?
- Use conjunctions: *und, aber, oder*.
- Use intensifiers: *sehr, ziemlich, ein bisschen, nicht so*.

5 Translate the sentences into German.

- a I have seven guinea pigs and six birds.
- b I have long black hair and brown eyes.
- c I have two stepsisters.
- d She is funny, energetic and positive.
- e He doesn't have any brothers or sisters.

6 Deine deutsche Freundin Lena fragt dich etwas über deinen Lieblingsschauspieler/deine Lieblingsschauspielerin (*your favourite actor*). Du schreibst Lena eine E-Mail.

Schreib:
- wie er/sie heißt
- wie alt er/sie ist und wann er/sie Geburtstag hat
- etwas über seine/ihre Haare und Augen
- etwas über seine/ihre Persönlichkeit.

Du musst ungefähr 40 Wörter auf Deutsch schreiben.

hunderteinunddreißig

3 Sprungbrett

🎧 Hören

1 〰️ Listen to three Austrian friends talking about what they do in their free time. Choose the correct activity (a, b, or c) for each person.

1 a b c

2 a b c

3 a b c

2 〰️ Listen to two Swiss teenagers talking about music. Complete the sentences in English.

1 Max says that he likes _____ .
2 Wali says that she prefers _____ .

3 〰️ Mehmet spricht über seine Freizeit. Hör zu und schreib den richtigen Buchstaben.

1 Wie oft spielt er Basketball?
   a jeden Tag
   b nie
   c einmal pro Woche
2 Was spielt er am liebsten?
   a Rugby
   b Fußball
   c Basketball

4 〰️ Ein Radiosprecher spricht über Jugendliche und Technologie. Hör zu und beantworte die Fragen auf Deutsch.

a Wie oft sind die meisten Jugendlichen online?
b Was machen sie am liebsten? (2 marks)
c Warum sehen sie nicht so gern fern?
d Was können Jugendliche machen, wenn sie nicht online sind? (3 marks)

> 💡 **Tipp**
>
> When tackling questions in German, you can use the question vocabulary to give you clues about what to listen out for.
>
> - Listen carefully for detail. The first suitable item you hear may not be the correct one!
> - Small, high-frequency words (*nicht, gern, aber,* etc.) can make all the difference to meaning.

hundertzweiunddreißig

3 Meine Freizeit

💬 Sprechen

5 Practise the role play.

Your teacher will play the part of your exchange partner and will speak first.

You should address your partner as *du*.

When you see this – ! – you will have to respond to something you have not prepared.

When you see this – ? – you will have to ask a question.

> Du sprichst mit deinem deutschen Austauschpartner/ deiner deutschen Austauschpartnerin über deine Freizeit.
> - Lieblingsaktivitäten
> - Meinung über Sport
> - !
> - Meinung über Musik
> - ?

6 Practise the photo card activity.

Look at the photo and prepare notes to answer the following questions.

- Was gibt es auf dem Foto?
- Spielst du ein Instrument?
- Was für Musik hörst du gern?

Think about any other questions you may be asked in relation to **free time and hobbies**.

Your teacher will ask you the three questions and then **two more questions** which you have not prepared.

💡 Tipp

Being able to talk confidently and spontaneously in German is a vital skill, both for any future exams and for building relationships. The more you practise, the more skilled you will become at saying exactly what you want.

- Use the vocabulary and structures you know as your starting point. It will be much easier than converting your thoughts from English into German.
- Give as much detail as you can. Include likes and dislikes, reasons (*denn...*), intensifiers (*ziemlich/ sehr*) and conjunctions (*und/aber*).
- Remember, it's OK to talk about what you don't know or haven't experienced, as long as you have something to say: what do you prefer to do instead?
- When you prepare a role play or photo card activity, try to predict questions on the topic, so that you have an answer ready.
- You can check you've understood by repeating part of the question back, e.g. *Meine Lieblingsmusik?* Don't be afraid to say *Noch einmal, bitte* or *Kannst du/ Können Sie das wiederholen?* if you'd like a question repeated.

7 Your teacher will ask you these questions. Answer them <u>without</u> making notes, using the language you already know.

- Was für Musik hörst du gern?
- Wie findest du YouTube-Stars?
- Hast du ein Handy? Was machst du damit?
- Spielst du ein Instrument? Bist du musikalisch?

hundertdreiunddreißig

4 Sprungbrett

Lesen

1 Read the forum contributions and answer the questions. Write S for Sophie, K for Karl, F for Fatimah, M for Matthias or J for Janina.

> Ich mag alle meine Fächer, aber besonders liebe ich Französisch und Spanisch, weil sie wichtig sind. **Sophie**

> Meine Schule ist im Zentrum von Wien. Die Klassenzimmer sind sehr klein. Das finde ich nicht gut, weil in meiner Klasse einunddreißig Schüler und Schülerinnen sind. **Karl**

> Ich interessiere mich für Natur, Tiere und Elektronik. Chemie, Physik und Biologie sind meine Lieblingsfächer. **Fatimah**

> Ich lerne jeden Tag viel. Jeden Dienstag und Donnerstag lerne ich nach der Schule mit Freunden. Das macht Spaß und ist effektiv. **Matthias**

> Ich bin nicht sehr gut organisiert! Manchmal bin ich in der Schule und mein Heft und Federtasche sind nicht in meiner Schultasche. **Janina**

a Who doesn't like his/her classroom?
b Who likes languages?
c Who likes studying science?
d Who sometimes doesn't have the right things in his/her school bag?
e Who enjoys learning in a group?
f Whose class has more than 30 students?

2 Lies Laras E-Mail. Wähl die <u>vier</u> richtigen Aussagen (*statements*).

Von: larascholte@g-online.at

Hallo Tom!

Ich schreibe heute über meine Schule. Ich gehe in ein Gymnasium und in fünf Jahren mache ich Matura. Ich gehe sehr gern in die Schule, weil sie nicht so groß ist. Die Lehrer sind alle sympathisch.

Die Schule beginnt um halb acht und das nervt, besonders im Winter. Ich habe jeden Tag eine Stunde Mathe. Das finde ich schwierig, aber der Lehrer ist nett und sehr hilfsbereit.

Am Montag gehe ich in die Theater-AG und am Mittwoch in den Chor. Das macht voll Spaß.

das Matura — Austrian equivalent of A levels

a	Lara geht in eine Gesamtschule.
b	Die Schule ist sehr groß.
c	Die Schule beginnt um 7:30.
d	Lara lernt jeden Tag Mathe.
e	Sie findet Mathe einfach.
f	Der Mathelehrer ist hilfsbereit.
g	Sie geht in eine AG dreimal pro Woche.
h	Einmal pro Woche geht sie in die Chor-AG.

3 Translate your Swiss exchange partner's message into English for your parents.

Ich gehe sehr gern in die Schule. Ich denke, alle meine Fächer sind wichtig und nützlich. Am liebsten mag ich Musik und Kunst, weil ich kreativ bin. Mein Musiklehrer ist ganz lustig und hilfsbereit und das finde ich prima.

4 In der Schule

✏️ Schreiben

4 **Du schickst dieses Foto an einen Freund in Österreich. Schreib vier Sätze auf Deutsch über das Foto.**

- Auf dem Foto gibt es… (eine Lehrerin/Schüler/Schülerinnen).
- Die Schüler lernen…
- Der Schüler im Vordergrund…
- Der Schüler im Hintergrund…
- Die Lehrerin…

💡 Tipp
Think about possible questions you could answer when writing sentences about the photo:
- Wie viele Schüler gibt es?
- Was lernen sie?
- Wo sind sie?
- Sieht die Lehrerin freundlich/hilfsbereit/sympathisch aus?
- Muss man hier eine Uniform tragen?

5 **Translate the sentences into German.**

a My favourite subject is geography.
b I don't like history.
c My teacher is very friendly.
d We have six lessons per day.
e I find my school rules very strict.

💡 Tipp
When you translate from English into German or German into English, don't forget to translate words like *sehr* (very) and *ziemlich* (quite), as they are easily forgotten. A grammar checklist can be really useful for checking your finished work. For example, check that you have used the correct genders for nouns and the correct pronouns for people (*ich*, *wir*, etc.), and make sure that your verb endings are accurate.

6 **Du schreibst an einen deutschen Freund über deine Schule.**

Schreib etwas über:
- deine Fächer
- deine Schulgebäude
- deine Lehrer
- die Schulregeln.

Du musst ungefähr 40 Wörter auf Deutsch schreiben.

hundertfünfunddreißig **135**

5 Sprungbrett

🎧 Hören

1 〰️ **Listen to three people discussing their food preferences. Copy and complete the table in English.**

	Likes (two details)	Dislikes	Reason for dislikes
1			
2			
3			

2 〰️ **Listen to Lutz talking about his diet. Which two food items are not mentioned?**

- a apples
- b oranges
- c eggs
- d bananas
- e pasta
- f water
- g plums
- h rice

3 〰️ **Axel isst im Restaurant. Hör zu und beantworte die Fragen.**

1. Was nimmt er als Hauptspeise?
   - a Hähnchen mit Reis
   - b Nudeln
   - c Pizza
2. Wie findet er das Essen?
   - a Es hat ihm geschmeckt.
   - b Es hat ihm gar nicht geschmeckt.
   - c Er hat es nicht gegessen.
3. Warum nimmt er keine Nachspeise? Beantworte die Frage auf Deutsch.

4 〰️ **Ein Ernährungsexperte spricht über Kinder und gesundes Essen. Hör zu und beantworte die Fragen auf Deutsch.**

- a Was sollen Eltern ihren Kindern erklären?
- b Was soll man zu Hause tun?
- c Was kann man mit Hähnchen essen? (4 marks)
- d Was passiert, wenn die Eltern den Kindern nur Pommes geben?

> 💡 **Tipp**
>
> Some questions award more than one mark for the answer.
> - Take note of these questions <u>before</u> listening. You will need to identify more than one piece of information.
> - Don't include irrelevant or unnecessary information in your response. If an answer awards three marks, only your first three details will be marked.

5 Mahlzeit!

💬 Sprechen

5 **Practise the role play.**

Your teacher will play the part of your friend and will speak first.

You should address your friend as *du*.

When you see this – ! – you will have to respond to something you have not prepared.

When you see this – ? – you will have to ask a question.

> Du sprichst mit deinem Freund/deiner Freundin über deinen Lebensstil.
> - Lieblingsessen
> - Tägliches Essen
> - !
> - Meinung über Junkfood
> - ?

6 **Practise the photo card activity.**

Look at the photo and prepare notes to answer the following questions.

- Was gibt es auf dem Foto?
- Was isst du zum Frühstück?
- Isst du gesund?

Think about any other questions you may be asked in relation to **healthy living**.

Your teacher will ask you the three questions and then **two more questions** which you have not prepared.

💡 Tipp

Speaking fluently matters, but so does accuracy. It might seem hard to combine the two, but it gets easier with practice.

- Take care with your tenses, listening carefully to the tenses used in any questions.
- Don't be afraid to correct yourself if you stumble over a sentence or use the wrong endings.
- Knowing the correct gender of nouns will make a huge difference when it comes to speaking fluently. Eventually, you will reach a stage where you don't have to think about it. In the meantime, take note of the gender each time you encounter a new piece of vocabulary.

7 **Your teacher will ask you these questions. Answer them <u>without</u> making notes, using the language you already know.**

- Isst du Junkfood? Warum (nicht)?
- Kochst du gern?
- Was ist deine Lieblingsmahlzeit?
- Was hast du gestern (*yesterday*) gegessen?

hundertsiebenunddreißig **137**

Grammatik

Nouns

The gender of nouns

There are three **genders** for nouns in German: masculine (*der*), feminine (*die*) and neuter (*das*).

It's best to try to learn any new nouns you encounter with their gender (and with their plural form). There are also a few guidelines to help you work out genders, although there are exceptions.

Have a look at these examples:

Masculine nouns include:	example
	der / ein
male people	Mann
seasons	Sommer
months	Mai
days	Freitag
compass points	Norden
most -en endings	Morgen
-ing endings	Frühling
-ig endings	König

Feminine nouns include:	example
	die / eine
female people	Frau
female people with -in endings	Lehrerin
most fruits	Erdbeere
-ung endings	Zeitung
-heit endings	Freiheit
-keit endings	Wirklichkeit
-schaft endings	Freundschaft
-ei endings	Bäckerei
-tät endings	Aktivität
-ik endings	Musik
many -e endings	Farbe

Neuter nouns include:	example
	das / ein
most countries	Deutschland
nouns formed from verbs	Lesen
-chen endings	Mädchen
-lein endings	Fräulein
most Ge- nouns	Getränk
most foreign words	Hotel

Definite and indefinite articles

The **definite articles** ('the') in German are *der* (m), *die* (f), *das* (n) in the singular. When nouns are plural, the definite article is *die*: *Hier sind die Kinder.*

The **indefinite articles** ('a/an') in German are *ein* (m), *eine* (f), *ein* (n). There is no plural form.

The word *kein* ('no/not any') is sometimes called the negative article. It follows the same pattern as *ein/eine/ein*, but its plural form is *keine*: *Sie haben keine Kinder.*

Grammatik

Plural nouns

If you want to use a German noun in the **plural** form (i.e. more than one), you'll need to know (or check) how that noun changes in the plural, as German has several different ways of making plurals.

In the dictionary, the plural form will be shown in brackets after the noun: *Banane (-n)*; *Tisch (-e)*; *Lehrer (–)*. The last of these (–) indicates no change in the plural.

Remember that a few nouns are always plural because of what they mean: *Eltern* (parents); *Großeltern* (grandparents); *Ferien* (holidays); *Leute* (people).

There are also some nouns which are never used in the plural because they are uncountable nouns. For example *der Kaffee* (coffee); *das Obst* (fruit); *das Wetter* (weather); *das Glück* (happiness/luck); *das Gepäck* (luggage).

Forming plural nouns

Here are some guidelines to help you learn patterns for forming plural nouns:

- A large number of **masculine** nouns add **-e** in the plural: *die Tage, die Monate, die Hunde*.
- A large number of **feminine** nouns form their plural with **-n**, **-en** or **-nen**: *die Schulen, die Lehrerinnen*. This includes all words ending in *-heit*, *-keit*, *-schaft* and *-ung*: *die Krankheiten, die Schwierigkeiten, die Freundschaften, die Zeitungen*.
- Some common **neuter** nouns add **-er**: *die Bilder, die Kleider*. Others do not change if they already end in *-er*, or if they end in *-chen* or *-lein*: *die Fenster, die Mädchen, die Männlein*.
- Many nouns gain an **-e** or an **-er** and an umlaut in their plural form: *die Hand → die Hände*; *der Gast → die Gäste*; *der Mann → die Männer*; *das Land → die Länder*.
- Nouns that end in -s (e.g. *der Bus*) often gain a second 's' in their plural ending: *die Busse*.
- Words of foreign origin (loan words) usually add -s: *die Sofas, die Büros*.

The case system

German articles change according to how they are used in a sentence. This is called the **case**.

There are four cases in German: nominative, accusative, dative and genitive.

The nominative and accusative cases

The **nominative** case is used for the subject of the sentence (the person doing the action of the verb). Here is an example:

Subject	Verb	
Das Mädchen	ist	lustig.

The **accusative** case is used for the direct object of the sentence (the person/thing which has the action done to it). Here is an example:

Subject	Verb	Direct object
Ich	habe	ein**en** Bruder.

Some **prepositions** (words like 'in', 'through', 'with', etc.) are also followed by the accusative case, such as *für* ('for'): *Ich habe ein**en** Kuchen für mein**en** Freund gebacken.* (I baked a cake for my friend.)

This is how the case system looks in the nominative and accusative cases, with both definite and indefinite articles. Note that the only change is in the masculine accusative:

	Definite articles			
	Masculine	Feminine	Neuter	Plural
Nominative	der Mann	die Frau	das Buch	die Far...
Accusative	**den** Mann	die Frau	das Buch	d...

	Indefinite articles		
	Masculine	Feminine	Neuter
Nominative	ein Mann	eine Frau	ein B...
Accusative	ein**en** Mann	eine Frau	

Remember that the **possessive adjec**... (the words for 'my', 'your', 'his', 'her', *ein* and *kein*, and so take the same...

Grammatik

Adjectives

Adjectives are words that describe nouns. When adjectives come <u>after</u> the noun, they behave just like English adjectives:

*Meine Mutter ist **freundlich**.*

*Die Fische sind **rot**.*

However, when adjectives come <u>before</u> the noun, you have to give them an ending.

Here are the adjective endings which are added when adjectives follow a definite article ('the') in the nominative and accusative cases. Note that the only change is in the masculine accusative.

	Definite articles			
	Masculine	**Feminine**	**Neuter**	**Plural**
Nominative	der groß**e** Vogel	die groß**e** Katze	das groß**e** Pferd	die groß**en** Giraffen
Accusative	den groß**en** Vogel	die groß**e** Katze	das groß**e** Pferd	die groß**en** Giraffen

Here are the adjective endings we add when adjectives follow an indefinite article ('a/an') or *kein* ('no/not any') in the nominative and accusative cases. The only change is in the masculine accusative.

Nominative

…re is no article before the noun and different …tive endings apply. For example, adjectives take …al noun when there is no article:

… schwarz**e** Haare.

Pronouns

Subject pronouns

Subject pronouns are the words for 'I', 'you', 'he', etc.

ich	I
du	you (familiar, singular)
er/sie/es	he/she/it
man	one, people, you, we (non-specific)
wir	we
ihr	you (familiar, plural)
Sie	you (formal, singular or plural)
sie	they

The subject pronoun *man* is used when you are not talking about anyone in particular and always takes the same form of the verb as *er*, *sie* and *es*:

Man *muss eine Uniform tragen.*
(We have to wear a uniform.)

When we use verbs, subject pronouns dictate how the verb should be formed.

Verbs

A **verb** is a word used to describe an action, and all sentences must contain one.

If you look up a verb in the dictionary, you will find it in its **infinitive** form with either an -*en* or -*n* at the end.

For each different person or pronoun (*ich*, *du*, *er*, etc.), you have to use the correct verb ending. Working out a verb's different forms is called **conjugation**.

Regular verbs in the present tense

Many German verbs follow the same pattern of conjugation: these are called **regular verbs**.

Regular verbs are formed by first removing the -*en* from the infinitive to find the verb 'stem', and then adding the correct ending to the stem.

Here is the verb *machen* ('to do/make') as an example:

machen
ich mach**e**
du mach**st**
er/sie/es mach**t**
wir mach**en**
ihr mach**t**
sie/Sie mach**en**

Irregular verbs in the present tense

Irregular verbs have the same endings as regular verbs BUT, in the *du* and *er/sie/es* forms, the vowel sound changes in the middle of the verb.

There are three ways for the vowel change to happen: the addition of an umlaut (*fahren*); the addition of an extra vowel (*sehen*); or the replacement of the original vowel with another one (*geben*):

Change a > ä e.g. **fahren**	Change e > ie e.g. **sehen**	Change e > i e.g. **geben**
ich fahre	ich sehe	ich gebe
du f**ä**hrst	du s**ie**hst	du g**i**bst
er/sie/es f**ä**hrt	er/sie/es s**ie**ht	er/sie/es g**i**bt

The present tense of *sein* ('to be') and *haben* ('to have')

The most common irregular verbs, *sein* and *haben*, do not follow the patterns of other irregular verbs, so it is important to learn these off by heart as soon as you can.

sein	haben
ich bin	ich habe
du bist	du hast
er/sie/es ist	er/sie/es hat
wir sind	wir haben
ihr seid	ihr habt
sie/Sie sind	sie/Sie haben

Using (gar nicht) gern, lieber and am liebsten

To say that you like doing something, you use *gern* straight after the verb. Depending on the degree of how much you like or dislike something you can use:

(gar) nicht gern	✗	indicates dislike
gern	✓	indicates like
lieber	✓✓	indicates preference
am liebsten	✓✓✓	indicates like best of all

Unlike in English, sentences with *gern* still use the same main verb – it's *gern*, *lieber* and *am liebsten* that change the meaning of the sentence. For example:

Ich schwimme gern.
(I like swimming.)

Ich mache lieber Yoga.
(I prefer doing yoga.)

Am liebsten lese ich.
(I like reading best of all./Most of all, I like reading.)

Grammatik

Modal verbs

Modal verbs are a group of verbs that typically express what we want to, can, should, must or may do. They include the verbs *sollen* (to ought/be supposed to), *können* (to be able to), *müssen* (to have to) and *dürfen* (to be allowed to).

When you use a modal verb, you need a second verb to complete the idea. This is similar to using another verb after 'I can…' in English. In German, the second verb goes to the end of the sentence and is given in the infinitive form.

Man kann jeden Dienstag in die Film-AG gehen.
(You can go to film club every Tuesday.)

Ich darf kein Make-up tragen.
(I'm not allowed to wear any make-up.)

The perfect tense with *haben*

The **perfect tense** is used to talk about things that happened in the past. It is made up of two parts: the **auxiliary** (or 'helping') verb and the **past participle**. The auxiliary verb goes in the usual place (second) and it is usually *haben*. The past participle goes at the end of the sentence.

To form the past participle, you remove the *-en* from the infinitive of the verb. Then you (usually) add *ge-* to the beginning of the verb stem and *-t* to the end:

ich **habe ge**spiel**t**	I played, I have played
du **hast ge**mach**t**	you did, you have done
er/sie/es **hat ge**kauf**t**	he/she/it bought, he/she/it has bought
wir **haben ge**spiel**t**	we played, we have played
ihr **habt ge**mach**t**	you did, you have done
sie/Sie **haben ge**kauf**t**	they/you bought, they/you have bought

Verbs which begin with certain **prefixes** do not add *ge-* to the past participle. These include **ver-** (e.g. *versuchen*), **be-** (e.g. *besuchen*) and **ge-** (e.g. *gewinnen*). Verbs which end in **-ieren** (e.g. *studieren*) also do not add *ge-*.

Word order

Basic word order

Here is the **basic word order** in a German sentence:

Subject	Verb	Rest of the sentence
Ich	gehe	ins Kino.

The verb-second rule

The **verb** is always in second place in a sentence or clause. This does not mean it is the second word but the **second idea**. Here is an example:

1st idea	2nd idea	Remaining idea
Meine Freundin	ist	intelligent.

Changing a sentence so that the subject is no longer the first idea is called using **inversion**. Inversion is used in the following sentence, where the first idea is an **adverb** of frequency ('sometimes'):

1st idea	2nd idea	Remaining ideas
Manchmal	sehe	ich fern.

Subordinate clauses

A **subordinate clause** is dependent on a main clause and does not make sense on its own, e.g. *weil es 10 Uhr ist* (because it is 10 o'clock).

The conjunction *weil* sends the verb to the end of the subordinate clause it introduces:

*Ich lerne gern Deutsch, weil es Spaß **macht**.*

Grammatik

Verb tables

Present tense

Regular verbs

wohnen ('to live')	**machen** ('to do/make')	**spielen** ('to play')	**lieben** ('to love')
ich wohne	ich mache	ich spiele	ich liebe
du wohnst	du machst	du spielst	du liebst
er/sie/es wohnt	er/sie/es macht	er/sie/es spielt	er/sie/es liebt
wir wohnen	wir machen	wir spielen	wir lieben
ihr wohnt	ihr macht	ihr spielt	ihr liebt
sie/Sie wohnen	sie/Sie machen	sie/Sie spielen	sie/Sie lieben

Irregular verbs

haben ('to have')	**sein** ('to be')
ich habe	ich bin
du hast	du bist
er/sie/es hat	er/sie/es ist
wir haben	wir sind
ihr habt	ihr seid
sie/Sie haben	sie/Sie sind

fahren ('to travel/ride (sth)')	**sehen** ('to see')	**essen** ('to eat')	**nehmen** ('to take')
ich fahre	ich sehe	ich esse	ich nehme
du fährst	du siehst	du isst	du nimmst
er/sie/es fährt	er/sie/es sieht	er/sie/es isst	er/sie/es nimmt
wir fahren	wir sehen	wir essen	wir nehmen
ihr fahrt	ihr seht	ihr esst	ihr nehmt
sie/Sie fahren	sie/Sie sehen	sie/Sie essen	sie/Sie nehmen

Perfect tense

wohnen ('to live')	**machen** ('to do/make')	**spielen** ('to play')
ich habe … gewohnt	ich habe … gemacht	ich habe … gespielt
du hast … gewohnt	du hast … gemacht	du hast … gespielt
er/sie/es hat … gewohnt	er/sie/es hat … gemacht	er/sie/es hat … gespielt
wir haben … gewohnt	wir haben … gemacht	wir haben … gespielt
ihr habt … gewohnt	ihr habt … gemacht	ihr habt … gespielt
sie/Sie haben … gewohnt	sie/Sie haben … gemacht	sie/Sie haben … gespielt

Glossar

Here is a key to the abbreviations used in the glossary:

- **adj** adjective – a describing word
- **adv** adverb – a word that describes or changes the meaning of a verb or adjective
- **conj** conjunction – a joining word
- **n** noun – a person, animal, object, place or thing
- **n pl** plural noun – a noun in the plural form (more than one)
- **p** preposition – a word that specifies time, direction or place
- **v** verb – a 'doing' or 'being' word

A

	ab und zu	adv	now and then
	abends	adv	in the evening
	am Abend	adv	in the evening
das	Abendessen (-)	n	evening meal, dinner
	zum Abendessen		for dinner
	aber	conj	but
	Abonnenten	n pl	subscribers
die	AG (-s) (= Arbeitsgemeinschaft)	n	after-school club
	Ich besuche die … -AG./ Ich gehe in die … -AG.		I go to … club.
	aggressiv	adj	aggressive
	alles		everything
	Ich esse alles.		I eat everything/anything.
	angeln gehen	v	to go fishing
	anstrengend	adj	tiring
die	Anti-Mobbing-AG (-s)	n	anti-bullying club
	April	n	April
der	Arm (-e)	n	arm
	asozial	adj	anti-social
die	Atmosphäre	n	atmosphere
	attraktiv	adj	attractive
	ätzend	adj	awful
	auch	conj	also
	August	n	August

die	Aula (Aulen)	n	(assembly) hall
die	ausgewogene Ernährung	n	balanced diet
	ausruhen	v	to relax
	auswendig lernen	v	to learn off by heart
der/die	Autor (-en)/Autorin (-nen)	n	author

B

das	Ballett	n	ballet
der	Bär (-en)	n	bear
der	Bart (Bärte)	n	beard
der	Basketball	n	basketball
die	Bastel-AG	n	crafts club
	basteln	v	to do crafts
der	Bauch (Bäuche)	n	stomach
die	Bedienung	n	service
das	Bein (-e)	n	leg
	(für…) bekannt	adj	known (for…)
	bekommen	v	to get, receive
	beliebt	adj	popular
der	Beruf (-e)	n	job/occupation
	berühmt	adj	famous
	bescheuert	adj	stupid
	besser essen	v	to eat better
das	Bild (-er)	n	photo, picture
die	Biologie	n	biology
	blau	adj	blue
	blond	adj	blond
	böse	adj	evil, bad
die	Bratwurst (-würste)	n	sausage
	braun	adj	brown
das	Brot	n	bread
das	Brötchen (-)	n	(bread) roll
der	Bruder (Brüder)	n	brother
	Ich habe einen Bruder.		I have a brother.
die	Butter	n	butter

C

	(mit Freunden) chatten	v	to chat/text (with friends)
die	Chemie	n	chemistry
	chillen	v	to relax
der	Chor (Chöre)	n	choir
	Ich gehe in den Chor.		I go to choir.
	cool	adj	cool

D

	danke		thank you
	dann	conj	then, next
	Das ist ein/eine/ein...		It's a...
	dein/deine	adj	your
der	Delphin (-e)	n	dolphin
	denn	conj	because
das	Deutsch	n	German
	Deutschland	n	Germany
	Dezember	n	December
	dick	adj	fat
das	Dorf (Dörfer)	n	village
die	Dose (-n)	n	can, tin

E

	egoistisch	adj	selfish
das	Eis	n	ice cream
das	Ei (-er)	n	egg
	ein bisschen		a bit
	einfach	adj	easy
	einkaufen gehen	v	to go shopping
	einmal pro Woche	adv	once a week
	Ich bin Einzelkind.		I'm an only child.
der	Elefant (-en)	n	elephant
die	elektronische Musik	n	electronic dance music, electronica
der	Ellenbogen (-)	n	elbow
	Eltern	n pl	parents
	energisch	adj	energetic
das	Englisch	n	English
	entdecken	v	to discover
	entspannend	adj	relaxing
die	Erdkunde	n	geography
die	Ernährung	n	diet
	Es gefällt mir nicht.		I don't like it.
	Es gefällt mir.		I like it.
	Es ist...		It is...
	Es kostet ... Euro/Cent.		It costs ... euros/cent.
	Es macht spaß.		It is fun.
	Es schmeckt mir/ Mir schmeckt's.		It tastes good.
	Ich esse ... mit...		I eat ... with...
	Etwas zu trinken?		(Would you like) anything to drink?

F

das	Fach (Fächer)	n	(school) subject
	fahren	v	to travel
die	Familie (-n)	n	family
das	Familienmodell (-e)	n	family structure
die	Familienzeit	n	family time
der	Fan (-s)	n	fan
die	Farbe (-n)	n	colour
das	Fastfood	n	fast food
	faszinierend	adj	fascinating
	faul	adj	lazy
	faulenzen	v	to lounge/laze about
	Februar	n	February
der	Federball	n	badminton
	fernsehen	v	to watch television
das	Fett (-e)	n	fat
die	Figur (-en)	n	character
die	Film-AG	n	film club
	finden	v	to find
der	Fisch	n	fish
	Ich esse kein Fisch.		I don't eat fish.
das	Fitnesscenter (-)	n	gym
der	Flammkuchen (-)	n	thin pizza
die	Flasche (-n)	n	bottle
das	Fleisch	n	meat
	Ich esse kein Fleisch.		I don't eat meat.
der	Flur (-e)	n	corridor
	im Flur rennen	v	to run in the corridor
	im Internet forschen	v	to do research online
das	Foto (-s)	n	photo
	Fragen stellen	v	to ask questions
das	Französisch	n	French
die	Frau (-en)	n	woman
	frech	adj	cheeky
	Fremdsprachen	n pl	foreign languages
	freundlich	adj	friendly
das	Frühstück	n	breakfast
	Ich esse kein Frühstück.		I don't eat breakfast.
	zum Frühstück		for breakfast
	Frühstücksflocken	n pl	breakfast cereal
der	Fuß (Füße)	n	foot
der	Fußball	n	football
die	Fußball-AG	n	football club

Glossar

G

	gar nicht		not at all
der	Geburtstag	n	birthday
	Ich habe am … Geburtstag.		My birthday is on the…
das	Gedicht (-e)	n	poem
	Mir gefallen Biologie und Chemie.		I like biology and chemistry.
	Mir gefällt Mathe.		I like maths.
	gehen	v	to go
die	Geige (-n)	n	violin
	gelb	adj	yellow
das	Gemüse	n	vegetables
die	Geschichte	n	(as a school subject) history
die	Geschichte (-n)	n	story
	Geschwister	n pl	siblings
	Ich habe keine Geschwister.		I have no brothers or sisters.
das	Gesicht (-er)	n	face
	gesund	adj, adv	healthy
	gesund leben	v	to live healthily
	gewinnen	v	to win
die	Giraffe (-n)	n	giraffe
die	Gitarre (-n)	n	guitar
	glatt	adj	straight
das	Gramm (-)	n	gram
	100 Gramm	n	100 grams
	grau	adj	grey
	groß	adj	big
	Großbritannien	n	Great Britain
	Großeltern	n pl	grandparents
die	Großmutter (-mütter)	n	grandmother
der	Großvater (-väter)	n	grandfather
	grün	adj	green
	gut	adj	good
	gut aussehend	adj	good-looking
	Guten Appetit!		Enjoy your meal!
die	Gymnastik	n	gymnastics

H

	haben	v	to have
der	Hafen (Häfen)	n	port
	halb neun/zehn/elf…		half past eight/nine/ten…
der	Halbbruder (-brüder)	n	half-brother
die	Halbschwester (-n)	n	half-sister
der	Hamburger (-)	n	burger
die	Hand (Hände)	n	hand
	das Handy benutzen	v	to use your mobile phone
	ein Handy haben	v	to have a mobile phone
	hart	adj	harsh
	Hast du ein Haustier?		Do you have a pet?
	Hast du eine große Familie?		Do you have a big family?
	Hast du Geschwister?		Do you have any brothers or sisters?
	Hast du Hunger?		Are you hungry?
	Ich hätte gern einen/eine/ein…		(about food/drink) I would like a…
das	Hauptgericht (-e)	n	main course
die	Hauptstadt (-städte)	n	capital city
	Hausaufgaben	n pl	homework
	Hausaufgaben machen	v	to do homework
die	Hausaufgaben-AG	n	homework club
das	Haustier (-e)	n	pet
	Ich habe kein Haustier.		I don't have a pet.
die	Haut	n	skin
	Ich heiße…		I'm called…/My name is…
	herzlich	adj, adv	warm
	heute		today
	hilfsbereit	adj	helpful
der	Hip-Hop	n	hip-hop
	(Musik) hören	v	to listen to (music)
	hören	v	to listen
	hübsch	adj	pretty
der	Hund (-e)	n	dog

I

die	Idee (-n)	n	idea
	idyllisch	adj	idyllic
der	Indie	n	indie music
die	Informatik	n	computing
die	Informatik-AG	n	computing club
der	Informatikraum (-räume)	n	computer room
	inspirierend	adj	inspiring
	intelligent	adj	intelligent
	interessant	adj	interesting
	Fremdsprachen interessieren mich.		Languages interest me.
	Deutsch interessiert mich.		German interests me.
	im Internet	adv	on the internet

Glossar

J

das	Jahr (-e)	n	year
	Ich bin ... Jahre alt.		I am ... years old.
	Januar	n	January
	jeden Abend	adv	every evening
	jeden Montag/Dienstag/Mittwoch…	adv	every Monday/Tuesday/Wednesday
	jeden Tag	adv	every day
	joggen	v	to jog
der	Joghurt (-)	n	yoghurt
der	Judo	n	judo
	Juli	n	July
	Juni	n	June

K

der	Kaffee (-s)	n	coffee
das	Kamel (-e)	n	camel
der	Kanarienvogel (-vögel)	n	canary
das	Kaninchen (-)	n	rabbit
die	Kantine (-n)	n	canteen
das	Karate	n	karate
die	Käse	n	cheese
die	Katze (-n)	n	cat
	Kaugummi kauen	v	to chew gum
	Kekse	n pl	biscuits
das	Kilogramm (-)	n	kilogram
	ins Kino gehen	v	to go to the cinema
	klasse	adj	great
die	Klasse (-n)	n	school year, form
	Ich gehe in die siebte/achte/neunte Klasse.		I am in Year 7/8/9.
die	Klassenfahrt (-en)	n	school trip
	Klassenfahrten machen	v	to go on school trips
der/die	Klassensprecher (-)/Klassensprecherin (-nen)	n	student representative, form representative
	einen Klassensprecher haben	v	to have a student representative
das	Klassenzimmer (-)	n	classroom
die	klassische Musik	n	classical music
das	Klavier (-e)	n	piano
die	Kleidung	n	clothes
	klein	adj	small
das	Knie (-)	n	knee
der	Knödel (-)	n	dumpling
	Kohlenhydrate	n pl	carbohydrates
	Ich komme aus...		I come from...
	kommen	v	to come
der/die	Komponist (-en)/Komponistin (-nen)	n	composer
der	Kopf (Köpfe)	n	head
	kreativ	adj	creative
die	Kunst	n	art
der/die	Künstler (-)/Künstlerin (-nen)	n	artist
	kurz	adj	short
	Kurzfilme	n pl	short films
die	Kurzgeschichte (-n)	n	short story

L

das	Labor (-s)	n	science lab
	lang	adj	long
	langweilig	adj	boring
das	Latein	n	Latin
	launisch	adj	moody
	lecker	adj	delicious
der/die	Lehrer (-)/Lehrerin (-nen)	n	teacher
das	Lehrerzimmer (-)	n	staff room
die	Leichtathletik-AG	n	athletics club
	lernen	v	to learn, to study
	lesen	v	to read
	lieber	adv	better
	Lieblings-		*(added to noun)* favourite
das	Lieblingsessen (-)	n	favourite food
das	Lieblingsfach (-fächer)	n	favourite subject
die	Lieblingsfarbe	n	favourite colour
das	Lieblingsgetränk (-e)	n	favourite drink
das	Lieblingsstück (-e)	n	favourite piece (of music)
	am liebsten	adv	best of all
das	Lied (-er)	n	song
	Liedtexte	n pl	song lyrics
	liken	v	to like *(on social media)*
der	Liter (-)	n	litre
	lockig	adj	curly
	lustig	adj	funny

Glossar

M

	machen	v	to make/do
das	Mädchen (-)	n	girl
	Ich mag/mag (gar) nicht…		I like/don't like (at all)…
	Mahlzeit!		Enjoy your meal!
die	Mahlzeit (-en)	n	meal(time)
	Mai	n	May
das	Make-up	n	make-up
	malen	v	to paint
	Man soll … essen/trinken.		You ought to eat/drink…
	manchmal	adv	sometimes
der	Mann (Männer)	n	man
das	Märchen (-)	n	fairy tale
die	Marmelade (-n)	n	jam
	März	n	March
die	Mathematik	n	maths
der/die	Mathematiker (-)/Mathematikerin (-nen)	n	mathematician
die	Maus (Mäuse)	n	mouse
das	Meerschweinchen (-)	n	guinea pig
	mega	adj	mega, super
	mein/meine		my
die	Meinung (-en)	n	opinion
die	Melodie (-n)	n	melody
die	Milch	n	milk
	Milchprodukte	n pl	dairy products
	Mineralstoffe	n pl	minerals
	mit	p	with
	mittags	adv	at lunchtime, at midday
das	Mittagessen	n	lunch
	zum Mittagessen		for lunch
die	Mittagspause (-n)	n	lunch break
	mittellang	adj	medium-length
	mobben	v	to bully
	Ich möchte einen/eine/ein…		(about food/drink) I would like a…
der	Monat (-e)	n	month
die	Musik	n	music
	Ich bin (nicht) musikalisch.		I am (not) musical.
die	Musikart (-en)	n	type of music
der/die	Musiker (-)/Musikerin (-nen)	n	musician
das	Musikinstrument (-e)	n	musical instrument
	muskulös	adj	muscular
das	Müsli	n	muesli
die	Mutter (Mütter)	n	mother

N

die	Nachhilfe	n	extra tuition
	am Nachmittag	adv	in the afternoon
	nachmittags	adv	in the afternoon
die	Nachspeise (-n)	n	dessert
der	Name (-n)	n	name
die	Nase (-n)	n	nose
	Naturwissenschaften	n pl	sciences
	negativ	adj	negative
	Ich nehme einen/eine/ein…		I'll take a…
	nervig	adj	annoying
	nett	adj	nice, friendly
	nicht schlecht	adj	not bad
	nicht so (gut)	adj	not very/so (good)
	nie	adv	never
	niedlich	adj	cute
	Noten	n pl	marks
	Notizen machen	v	to make notes
	November	n	November
	Nudeln	n pl	pasta
	nur		only
	nützlich	adj	useful

O

das	Obst	n	fruit
	oder	conj	or
	oft	adv	often
	ohne	p	without
das	Ohr (-en)	n	ear
	Oktober	n	October
die	Oma (-s)	n	grandmother
das	Omelett (-s/-en)	n	omelette
	online sein	v	to be/go online
	ein Online-Profil haben	v	to have a profile online (on a social network)
der	Opa (-s)	n	grandfather
	optimistisch	adj	optimistic
	orange	adj	orange
der	Orang-Utan (-s)	n	orangutan
der	Ort (-e)	n	place
	Österreich	n	Austria

P

	ein paar		a few, some
die	Packung (-en)	n	packet
das	Panda (-s)	n	panda
die	Patchworkfamilie (-n)	n	blended family
die	Pause (-n)	n	break
	perfekt	adj	perfect
das	Pferd (-e)	n	horse
die	Physik	n	physics
der/die	Physiker (-)/Physikerin (-nen)	n	physicist
der	Pinguin (-e)	n	penguin
die	Pizza (-s)	n	pizza
	Pommes	n pl	chips
der	Pop	n	pop music
	populär	adj	popular
	positiv	adj	positive
	praktisch	adj	practical
der	Preis (-e)	n	price
	prima	adj	great
der	Prinz (-en)	n	prince
die	Prinzessin (-nen)	n	princess
	pummelig	adj	chubby
	pünktlich sein	v	to be punctual/on time

R

	Rad fahren	v	to ride a bike, to cycle
der	Rap	n	rap
der/die	Rapper (-)/Rapperin (-nen)	n	rapper
die	Ratte (-n)	n	rat
die	Regel (-n)	n	rule
	regelmäßig	adj	regularly
die	Regenbogenfamilie (-n)	n	rainbow family
der	Reis	n	rice
	respektvoll	adj	respectful
das	Restaurant (-s)	n	restaurant
die	Restaurantbewertung (-en)	n	restaurant review
der	Rock	n	rock music
der	Roman (-e)	n	novel
	rosa	adj	pink
	rot	adj	red
der	Rücken (-)	n	back
das	Rugby		rugby

S

der	Saft (Säfte)	n	juice
die	Sahne	n	cream
der	Salat (-e)	n	salad
	sammeln	v	to collect
der/die	Sänger (-e)/Sängerin (-nen)	n	singer
die	Schach-AG	n	chess club
die	Scheibe (-n)	n	slice
der	Schinken	n	ham
der	Schlager	n	German pop
das	Schlagzeug	n	drums
die	Schlange (-n)	n	snake
	schlank	adj	thin
das	Schloss (Schlösser)	n	castle
	schmecken	v	to taste good, to be tasty
	...schmeckt mir (nicht).		(about food/drink) I (don't) like...
	Schmeckt's dir?/Schmeckt es dir?		Does that taste good?/Do you find it tasty?
das	Schnitzel (-)	n	escalope, cutlet
der	Schnurrbart (-bärte)	n	moustache
	schön	adj	beautiful
	schrecklich	adj	awful
	schreiben	v	to write
	schüchtern	adj	shy
die	Schularbeit	n	school work
das	Schulfach (-fächer)	n	(school) subject
der	Schulhof (-höfe)	n	playground, school yard
	Schulrechte	n pl	school rights
	Schulregeln	n pl	school rules
der	Schulter (-n)	n	shoulder
die	Schuluniform (-en)	n	school uniform
	Ich bin schwach in...		I am bad at...
	schwarz	adj	black
die	Schweiz	n	Switzerland
die	Schwester (-n)	n	sister
	Ich habe eine Schwester.		I have a sister.
	schwierig	adj	difficult
	schwimmen	v	to swim
	sehen	v	to see/watch
	sehr		very
	sein	v	to be
das	Sekretariat	n	admin office, secretary's office
	Selfies machen	v	to take selfies
	selten	adv	rarely
der	Sender (-)	n	radio station

Glossar

	September	n	September
	singen	v	to sing
	skandalös	adj	scandalous
	Skateboard fahren	v	to go skateboarding
	Sketche	n pl	sketches
	Ski fahren	v	to ski
	Snowboard fahren	v	to snowboard
das	Soda (-)	n	fizzy drink
	Sommersprossen	n pl	freckles
der	Song (-s)	n	song
	Sonst noch was?		(Can I get you) anything else?
	soziale Medien	n pl	social media
die	Sozialkunde	n	social studies
das	Spanisch	n	Spanish
	spannend	adj	exciting
	spicken	v	to cheat
	spielen	v	to play
	Spielst du ein Instrument?		Do you play an instrument?
der	Sport (-e)	n	sport, PE
die	Sportart (-en)	n	type of sport
die	Sporthalle (-n)	n	sports hall
der/die	Sportler (-)/Sportlerin (-nen)	n	sportsperson
	Sport treiben	v	to do sport
die	Stadt (Städte)	n	town
	Ich bin stark in…		I am good at…
der	Stiefbruder (-brüder)	n	stepbrother
die	Stiefmutter (-mütter)	n	stepmother
die	Stiefschwester (-n)	n	stepsister
der	Stiefvater (-väter)	n	stepfather
die	Stimme (-n)	n	voice
die	Streetdance-AG	n	streetdance club
	streng	adj	strict
das	Stück (-e)	n	piece
	studieren	v	to study
die	Stunde (-n)	n	lesson
der	Stundenplan (-pläne)	n	timetable
die	Suppe (-n)	n	soup
	süße Getränke	n pl	sugary drinks
	sympathisch	adj	kind

T

die	Tafel (Täfeln)	n	bar
das	Tagebuch (-bücher)	n	diary
	täglich	adv	every day
	tanzen	v	to dance
der	Techno	n	techno
der	Tee (-s)	n	tea
	teilen	v	to share
das	Tennis	n	tennis
der	Text (-e)	n	text
die	Theater-AG	n	drama/theatre club
das	Theaterstück (-e)	n	play
das	Tier (-e)	n	animal
	toll	adj	great
die	Torte (-n)	n	tart
	total		totally
	tragen	v	to wear
	Treibst du Sport?		Do you do sport?
	treu	adj	loyal
	trinken	v	to drink
die	Trompete (-n)	n	trumpet
die	Tüte (-n)	n	bag (e.g. of sweets)
	typisch	adj	typical

U

	um … Uhr		at … o'clock
die	Umwelt-AG	n	environmental action group
	und	conj	and
	unfreundlich	adj	unfriendly
	ungemütlich	adj	uncomfortable
	im Unterricht	adv	in class
	unwichtig	adj	unimportant

V

der	Vater (Väter)	n	father
der/die	Veganer (-)/Veganerin (-nen)	n	vegan
der/die	Vegetarier (-)/Vegetarierin (-nen)	n	vegetarian
	verbringen	v	to spend (time)
der/die	Vertrauenslehrer (-)/Vertrauenslehrerin (-nen)	n	teacher who helps with student welfare, 'teacher you trust'
	mit dem Vertrauenslehrer sprechen	v	to speak with the student welfare teacher
	Videoclips sehen	v	to watch video clips
der/die	Videoproduzent (-en)/Videoproduzentin (-nen)	n	video producer/vlogger

Glossar

	Videos	n pl	videos
	Videospiele spielen	v	to play video games
	viel		a lot of
	vielleicht	adv	perhaps
	Viertel nach		quarter past (the hour)
	Viertel vor		quarter to (the hour)
	violett	adj	purple
	Vitamine	n pl	vitamins
	Vokabeln lernen	v	to learn vocabulary
	voll		really
	von … bis…		from … to…
die	Vorspeise (-n)	n	starter

W

der	Walross (Walrosse)	n	walrus
	Wann hast du Geburtstag?		When is your birthday?
	Was bist du/sind Sie von Beruf?		What is your job?
	Was darf es sein?		What would you like (to order/buy)?
	Was gibt es in deiner Schule?		What is there in your school?
	Was hast du am Montag?		What (lessons) do you have on Monday?
	Was isst du zum Frühstück/Mittagessen/Abendessen?		What do you eat for breakfast/lunch/evening meal?
	Was kostet das?		What does that cost?
	Was machst du in deiner Freizeit?		What do you do in your free time?
	Was machst du nach der Schule?		What do you do after school?
	Was nimmst du?		What are you having?/What will you have?
	Was trinkst du zum Frühstück/Mittagessen/Abendessen?		What do you drink for breakfast/lunch/evening meal?
das	Wasser	n	water
	Wasser trinken	v	to drink water
	weil	conj	because
	weiß	adj	white
	Welche AG machst du?		Which after-school club do you go to?
	Welche Sportarten machst du?		Which sports do you do?
	wenig		little, a little of, not much
das	Werken	n	design and technology
	wichtig	adj	important
	Wie alt bist du?		How old are you?
	Wie findest du…?		How do you find…?
	Wie geht's?		How are you?
	Wie heißt du?		What's your name?
	Wie ist dein bester Freund/deine beste Freundin?		What's your best friend like?
	Wie sagt man…?		How do you say…?
	Wie schmeckt's?		How does it taste?
	Wie schreibt man das?		How do you write it?
	Wie siehst du aus?		What do you look like?
	Wie sieht er/sie aus?		What does he/she look like?
	Wie sind deine Augen?		What are your eyes like?
	Wie sind deine Haare?		What is your hair like?
das	Wochenende	n	weekend
	am Wochenende	adv	at the weekend
	Ich wohne in…		I live in…
	Wo wohnst du?		Where do you live?
	wohnen	v	to live (in a place)
der	Wohnort (-e)	n	place of residence
der	Wolf (Wölfe)	n	wolf
die	Wurst (Würste)	n	sausage

Y

der/das	Yoga	n	yoga

Z

	ziemlich		quite
	zocken	v	to game/play video games
der	Zucker	n	sugar
	zuhause bleiben	v	to stay at home
	zum Beispiel		for example
	zusammen leben	v	to live together
	zweimal pro Woche	adv	twice a week
die	Zwiebel (-n)	n	onion
	Zwillinge	n pl	twins
der	Zwillingsbruder (-brüder)	n	twin brother
die	Zwillingsschwester (-n)	n	twin sister

hunderteinundfünfzig

OXFORD
UNIVERSITY PRESS

Great Clarendon Street, Oxford, OX2 6DP, United Kingdom

Oxford University Press is a department of the University of Oxford. It furthers the University's objective of excellence in research, scholarship, and education by publishing worldwide. Oxford is a registered trade mark of Oxford University Press in the UK and in certain other countries

© Oxford University Press 2020

The moral rights of the authors have been asserted

First published in 2020

All rights reserved. No part of this publication may be reproduced, stored in a retrieval system, or transmitted, in any form or by any means, without the prior permission in writing of Oxford University Press, or as expressly permitted by law, by licence or under terms agreed with the appropriate reprographics rights organization. Enquiries concerning reproduction outside the scope of the above should be sent to the Rights Department, Oxford University Press, at the address above.

You must not circulate this work in any other form and you must impose this same condition on any acquirer

British Library Cataloguing in Publication Data
Data available

978-0-19-849471-3

10 9 8 7 6 5 4 3 2 1

Paper used in the production of this book is a natural, recyclable product made from wood grown in sustainable forests.

The manufacturing process conforms to the environmental regulations of the country of origin.

Printed in Great Britain by Bell and Bain Ltd., Glasgow

Acknowledgements

The publisher and authors would like to thank the following for permission to use photographs and other copyright material:

Cover (top to bottom): manfredxy/Shutterstock; Kiev.Victor/Shutterstock; Nikolai Tsvetkov/Shutterstock; whitelook/Shutterstock. All other photos © Shutterstock, except: **p8(bm):** mauritius images GmbH/Alamy Stock Photo; **p18(b):** Keystone Press/Alamy Stock Photo; **p20(t):** dpa picture alliance/Alamy Stock Photo; **p20(b):** Metzgerei_Zimmer/Bratwursthotel; **p21(tr):** ullstein bild/Getty Images; **p33(b):** Artexplorer/Alamy Stock Photo; **p35:** Everett Collection Inc/Alamy Stock Photo; **p37:** Everett Collection Inc/Alamy Stock Photo; **p41(b):** Historical image collection by Bildagentur-online/Alamy Stock Photo; **p42:** dpa picture alliance archive/Alamy Stock Photo; **p42(bl):** © Breathing Books 2016; **p42 (br):** © Cornelia Funke 2003; **p43(l, m):** Janosch film & medien AG; **p55:** Mark Bassett/OUP; **p62:** HMP/Alamy Stock Photo; **p63:** WENN Rights Ltd/Alamy Stock Photo; **p64(l):** The Goldfish, 1925 (no 86) (oil and w/c on paper on cardboard), Klee, Paul (1879-1940)/Hamburger Kunsthalle, Hamburg, Germany/Gift of Friends of Carl Georg Heises/Bridgeman Images; **p64(m):** European Holding Himself by his Moustache; Europaer Der Sich Seinem Schnurbart Halt, 1951 (watercolour on brown packing paper mounted on canvas), Hundertwasser, Friedensreich (1928-2000)/Private Collection/Photo © Christie's Images/Bridgeman Images; **p64(r):** Self Portrait at the Age of Twenty-Eight, 1500 (oil on panel), Dürer or Duerer, Albrecht (1471-1528)/Alte Pinakothek, Munich, Germany/Bridgeman Images; **p65:** dpa picture alliance/Alamy Stock Photo; **p81:** OUP/Chris King; **p96:** © Alamy Ltd/OUP; **p96:** Getty Photodisc/OUP; **p96(bl, br):** 123rf; **p99(t):** Juice Images/Alamy Stock Photo; **p99(b):** Getty Photodisc/OUP; **p109(b):** © Alamy Ltd/OUP; **p113:** © Alamy Ltd/OUP; **p115:** Mariia Boiko/Alamy Stock Photo; **p118(t):** Phil Wills/Alamy Stock Photo; **p118 (clock wise from top):** dpa picture alliance/Alamy Stock Photo; Leonardo Cendamo/Getty Images; Historical Picture Archive/Alamy Stock Photo; dpa picture alliance/Alamy Stock Photo. **p120(bl):** dpa picture alliance/Alamy Stock Photo; **p120(br):** Chronicle/Alamy Stock Photo; **p121(t):** INTERFOTO/Alamy Stock Photo; **p124:** Miquel Benitez/Shutterstock; **p125(t):** United Archives GmbH/Alamy Stock Photo; **p125(b):** Zoonar GmbH/Alamy Stock Photo; **p127(b):** UtCon Collection/Alamy Stock Photo; **p132:** Gareth Boden/OUP; **p132:** © Alamy Ltd/OUP; **p137:** Lev Dolgachov/Alamy Stock Photo.

Artwork by QBS Media Service Inc., except: Liz Kay **(p4-5, 30)**; Jordan Kincaid **(p11, 32, 122, 123, 127)**; Szilvia Szakall **(p38)**; Matt Ward **(p19, 54, 70, 80, 84, 101, 108)**; Joseph Wilkins **(p52, 74, 82, 98, 100, 102)**.

Page design by Kamae Design

The publisher and authors are grateful to the following for permission to reprint extracts from copyright material:

p42: https://www.cornelia-funke-baumhaus.de, reproduced with permission from Cornelia Funke; **p58:** https://www.unicef.de, reproduced with permission from the German Committee for UNICEF. Source: Schule ist Vollzeitjob für Kinder, Deutsches Kinderhilfswerk und UNICEF Veröffentlichen Umfrageergebnis

Audio recordings produced by Colette Thomson for Footsteps Productions Ltd and Andrew Garratt (sound engineer).

Although we have made every effort to trace and contact all copyright holders before publication this has not been possible in all cases. If notified, the publisher will rectify any errors or omissions at the earliest opportunity.

Links to third party websites are provided by Oxford in good faith and for information only. Oxford disclaims any responsibility for the materials contained in any third party website referenced in this work.